To Joyce & Kay

with fond regards

Joe

PSYCHOTHERAPY AND CHARACTER STRUCTURE

How to Recognize and Treat Particular Character Types

PSYCHOTHERAPY AND CHARACTER STRUCTURE

How to Recognize and Treat Particular Character Types

Mary Ahern, M.S.W., Ph.D.

University of California at San Francisco
San Francisco, California
and California Institute for Clinical Social Work
Berkeley, California

and

A. J. Malerstein, M.D.

University of California, Davis Medical Center
Sacramento, California

 **HUMAN SCIENCES PRESS, INC.**

Library of Congress Cataloging in Publication Data

Ahern, Mary.
    Psychotherapy and character structure: how to recognize and treat particular
character types / Mary Ahern, A. J. Malerstein.
        p.   cm.
    Bibliography: p.
    Includes index.
    ISBN 0-89885-466-0
    1. Psychotherapy. 2. Typology (Psychology) 3. Psychotherapist and patient. I.
Malerstein, A. J. (Abraham J.) II. Title.
    [DNLM: 1. Character. 2. Psychotherapy—methods. WM 420 A285p]
RC489.T95A37   1989
616.89'14—dc19
DNLM/DLC   88-28407
for Library of Congress   CIP

© 1989 Mary Ahern and A. J. Malerstein
Human Sciences Press, Inc., is a subsidiary of
Plenum Publishing Corporation
233 Spring Street, New York, N.Y. 10013

PREFACE

Over the years we have known a number of gifted therapists. Their solutions for particular patients were occasionally difficult to systematize. Some of these therapists were
exponents of a particular school of psychotherapy such as
behavior modification or psychoanalysis. Their therapeutic interventions, however, did not always fit the treatment approach of their school. It was unclear to us and
sometimes to the therapists themselves how they arrived
at the particular interventions they used, yet these interventions worked.

For example, Norman Reider recounted his treatment
of a couple, both members of which were psychotic. He
spoke to each separately, advising each that the spouse
was near becoming quite ill and that he or she should be
very gentle with the other. This intervention owed nothing to Reider's Freudian orientation. Yet we have little
doubt that his effort was helpful to these patients.

Perhaps these types of interventions will defy system-
atization and will always be relegated to the art of psychotherapy. We think, however, that our conceptualization of
character structure provides a rationale for some of these
treatment techniques and helps generate interventions

that serve the patient as he is—a person who may not fit the therapist's particular school of therapy.

This book is the last in a series of three in which we adopt and adapt Piaget's work in order to provide a new theory for understanding clinical practice and to propose some links between psychology and brain function (Malerstein and Ahern, 1982; Malerstein, 1986). We think Piaget's findings and his structural–constructivist theory provide the only system with some promise as a general psychology that embraces the complexities of biological, clinical, and normal psychology.

Principally this is a how-to book explaining how to recognize a particular character structure type, and how to make use of this recognition of character structure in treatment. We hope our treatment recommendations will be useful to other clinicians.

Mary Ahern
A. J. Malerstein

ACKNOWLEDGMENTS

We wish to thank Cynthia Hall for her editorial assistance, and Pamela J. Baird and René Hall for manuscript preparation. We are indebted to Arnold Meadow for his critique of our manuscript.

We failed to thank a number of people who helped us with our first book, *A Piagetian Model of Character Structure.* We would like to thank them now. Eleanor Duckworth helped us to avoid serious misinterpretations of Piaget's work. Rheta deVries generously let us use her translation of Piaget's notes for his course on affect given at the Sorbonne, which only later became generally available when published as *Intelligence and Affectivity* (1981). We are also grateful to Shirley Cooper, William Henry, Joan Martin, and Eric Wanner for their editorial suggestions at different stages in our many rewritings of the manuscript.

CONTENTS

PART III. TREATMENT

PART IV. THEORETICAL CONSIDERATIONS

Part I

A CHARACTER-CENTERED THEORY
OF PSYCHOTHERAPY

Chapter 1

INTRODUCTION

An associate of Frank Oppenheimer's, asking him to be practical, said "But Frank, we live in the real world." He responded, "No we don't. We live in a world we made up" (Murphy, 1985).

Born into a world that was constructed by those who went before him, a child has the remarkable ability to construct an understanding of the particular world he arrives in as he interacts with it—to see what works or, as in a severely psychotic person, to see if even anything works for him at all. If someone is born into a society in which there are no machines, then movement, as an attribute, is never split away from animal objects. Animals move; the rest does not. Therefore all things that move are animals. Clouds and the moon are animals; they move. The reasoning is correct for the world with which that person interacts. It is correct for early cultures as it is for young children.

Not only is the child adaptable but whatever he is born into—the raw material out of which he constructs his world—feels entirely natural to him. It is not surprising that later, when he has constructed his world out of his interaction with the particular raw material or nutrients provided him, he giggles while listening to strange (to him) sounds. When English has become the natural and normal language to speak, Hebrew sounds funny. A child learns to understand Cantonese or French, to use a tortilla or a spoon, to listen to stories, or to watch TV. Truly amazing is the adaptability of the child.

His initial adaptive possibilities are, however, not infinite. They are restricted by the nature, organization, and number of his physical parts, e.g., neurons, muscles, sensory organs, as well as by the attributes, including the history and instrumentation, of his part of this planet in its time frame. Nevertheless, the possibilities are many and varied. Yet to each growing child, the particular possibilities he has actuated are natural and normal. To each child these possibilities are the way things are. They are the way human beings are, including the way he is as a person. It is usually only later, during adolescence, that he realizes there are possibilities other than his way or his family's way.

During and after adolescence certain types of adaptability are lost. Generally, the postadolescent has great difficulty learning a new language. If he learns a new language, he as well as native speakers recognize that this language is not natural to him. So it is with character structure as we have defined it in our previous work (Malerstein & Ahern, 1982). Character structure in an adult does not basically change as a result of teaching or treatment. This does not mean we think that character structure is not modifiable at all or that no aspects of a person's makeup may alter with treatment. We think it is best during treatment to keep in mind that you can teach an adult new tricks, but you cannot teach him these tricks in the same way you could have when he was a youngster. Of course, when he was a child there were some tricks he could not have learned since he was not yet ready. We suggest that you have a better chance of teaching a person or of having him learn, that is teach himself, if you meet him where he is.

In this book we emphasize a theory of psychotherapy that adheres to the fundamental precept that the therapist should meet the patient where he is. Meeting the person where he is is not a new concept. Good teachers have used it all along (Duckworth, 1983). It fits the psychoanalytic dictum: start at the surface. Stress on empathy got new emphasis from Kohut (1977), and more recently from Havens (1986), although it was always a part of good psychotherapy and psychoanalysis. Meeting the client where he is is consonant with fundamental social work principles (Garrett, 1942), as well as with the theoretical concept emphasized by Piaget (1962) that an organism assimilates what it can at the level it can depending on the particular structures it has. If an adult speaks French then, all things being equal, it is easier for him to learn to drive a car from a driving instructor who speaks French, although that does not mean he cannot learn what he needs to know from someone who cannot speak at all. At least as much as speaking the same language, an instructor needs to know the quality of the student's grasp of driving a car and most of all how the student best learns, although the student may learn even with the additional burden of deciphering the driving instructor's language and teaching style.

Of the psychotherapy methods or systems in the existing literature, we discuss those that we think best fit a given character structure. We think a treatment approach should be fitted to the patient rather than the patient fitted to the treatment. Although we discuss a few new treatment techniques and offer our own reasons for selecting certain techniques and approaches, we do not introduce a new system of psychotherapy.

Integral to our goal of meeting the patient where he is, is our emphasis on the therapeutic relationship. The therapeutic relationship is an overall environmental system that is there throughout therapy. It is not just an interpretation, a few words, or some working through. Its effect on an individual in therapy is comparable to that of climate, day length, or food supply on a culture. We think the appropriate relationship carries the therapy, motivates the patient, and makes him willing to stay. It gives the patient a sense of being not in a foreign land, not an alien, not in dangerous territory.

We will also deal with what we have learned in the last 10 years as we used our model of character structure in supervision of treatment and in our own treatment of patients. Though we have not substantially altered our model, we have learned several things as we applied it to understanding both patients and nonpatients. We have found several adaptations to identity problems which we had not anticipated. We had thought that diagnosis of character structure was straightforward, but discovered that, although it was our own system, we each took a different approach to diagnosis of a person's character structure.

We had not initially intended to write a book on the application of our model to psychotherapy, because the basic psychotherapeutic approaches appropriate for our different character structures are already in the literature and because we assumed that selection of an appropriate approach would follow easily from an understanding of the patient's character structure. One clinician, who attempts to direct treatment toward insight, however, assumed the best use of our theory was to give every patient insight into his character structure. This is not what we expected. We especially wish to stress that no one treatment approach (e.g., psychoanalysis, cognitive therapy, or behavior modification) is suitable for all character types. We feel that knowledge of character structure provides a guide for selecting treatment approaches.

Given our definition of character structure as a person's most basic and abiding qualities, then "meeting the person where he is" means that treatment interventions along with the abiding stance taken by the therapist should be chosen with the patient's character structure in mind. Furthermore, it should be recognized that patients generally process experiences with a psychotherapist in the same way they process experiences with other persons, that is, basically in keeping with their character structure. This takes place whether or not the therapist is aware of it.

In Chapters 2, 3, and 4 we give a flavor of our goals in treatment. Although our theory of psychotherapy is character-centered, we recommend that an individual treatment plan be made for each patient. But since our theory of psychotherapy is based on who the patient is characterologically, an understanding of character structure is essential. Hence we review our model of character structure in Chapter 5 and our three character types in Chapter 6. A more complete description of the conceptualization of character structure is given in our first book (Malerstein & Ahern, 1982). We discuss diagnosis of character structure in Chapters 7 and 8. In Chapter 9 we focus on the therapeutic relationship, which we believe to be the most important psychotherapeutic lever. After we discuss treatment approaches to character structure in the next three chapters, in Chapter 13 we comment on treatment issues apart from those related to character structure. In Chapter 14 we assess what is altered in the course of treatment and how it is altered. Finally in Chapter 15 we suggest how newer findings in child development are accommodated by Piaget's system.

There are fundamental differences between a character-centered approach, such as ours, and a method-centered or person-centered approach. Implicit in a method-centered approach is the concept that illness and wellness lie on a single continuum, with illness, sometimes thought of as primitivity, at one end and wellness, sometimes thought of as maturity, at the other end. It then follows that a single method should move any patient along the continuum although sometimes certain modifications must be introduced to accommodate the degree of illness of a particular patient.

At the opposite pole from any method-centered approach is the person-centered approach, which assumes that each patient is unique and is entitled to be responded to as such, that a person may not be categorized, classified, or even diagnosed, lest his uniqueness be lost sight of. The person-centered approach cautions against a "cookbook" approach for fear that the nuances or even the essence of the patient might go unrecognized and full self-actualization might thus never be attained. (Oddly enough, this extreme form of person-centered approach sends a standard message that every person is very special. This supportive message undoubtedly is usually helpful.)

In our character-centered approach the belief is that each person, although unique in many ways, shares certain qualities with a group. Once a patient's membership in that group is recognized certain givens may be assumed. Although there is much to the person-centered approach, carried to an extreme it suggests there is no point in training psychotherapists but only in finding those therapists who are sensitive to the concepts and feelings of others. There is, of course, little doubt that some shared attitudes and empathy between therapist and patient are extremely important.

We believe that character structure becomes set during, and most likely toward the end of, the concrete operational period (8 to 11 years); such a fixity implies certain limits to psychotherapeutic effects. Trying to change a patient from one character structure to another is not productive. In addition, we do not think that the different character structures are pathologic per se. Accordingly, changing a patient from one character structure to another, were it possible, would to us not be desirable. This position conflicts with much of the literature dealing with character structure and treatment.

We will speak often in terms of brief therapy—reparative, not reconstructive, therapy. We will suggest there are particular patients, and patients in particular circumstances, even good analysands, for whom major reconstructive therapy is not appropriate.

Chapter 2

A PERSPECTIVE ON TREATMENT

ADDRESSING A SMALL ISSUE IN TREATMENT

In the course of treatment one encounters discrepancies between what a patient says one time and the next time, sometimes in the same hour, and discrepancies between the versions of a story told to different people. In classic uncovering psychotherapy, focus on such inconsistencies proves to be invaluable. If one explores these discrepancies fully, both sides of the story become understandable.

At a case conference we attended in Philadelphia discussion centered around how to handle one such discrepancy as presented by Mr. C. Mr. C, a self-taught auto mechanic promoted to auto parts sales, came for treatment of panics, which he referred to at different times as "fear of death," "dissolution," and "loss of identity." His first panic had occurred one year earlier, after his "rather aggressive" lover initiated a separation. His lover thought Mr. C had been too clinging.

After his lover left, Mr. C felt so relieved that while out running, he experienced a sense of "total freedom." The freedom was so great that he went into "overdrive" and experienced panic. Since then panics recurred, and with increasing frequency. His phobias spread to include fears of flying, of crossing bridges, and of walking along the street. He was able to get to work and home by parking directly in front of his house and place of work. "Not good about details," he forgot to move his car or feed the meter. A thousand dollars of parking tickets per month was to him an expectable "business" expense.

He was the middle child of three boys. He recounted that at age two he climbed on his grandmother's lap and said, "Don't leave me." His grandmother died shortly thereafter. His father became ill when Mr. C was in his early teens and died when Mr. C was 18. Mr. C regretted his "delinquency," that is, his cutting school, his not studying, and his daydreaming during his father's illness. After Mr. C's father's death, Mr. C's mother became very dependent upon him; the specifics and duration of this dependency were not described. In school he had difficulty with mathematics because he was "too distractible" to catch all the "details." He grasped literature and social history without having to be cognizant of all the details. Nonetheless he dropped out of college because of his distractibility.

Over 3 months of treatment with a warm, nonjudgmental therapist, he experienced no panics. He continued to see his general physician fairly often for nonserious physical complaints. The patient kept all appointments with the psychotherapist except the one just before the therapist's vacation, which the patient "forgot." Upon the therapist's return, the patient reported he still had had no panics. The therapist, however, discovered from reading the patient's medical chart, which included the general physician's notes, that the patient was panic-free until the time of the therapist's vacation, but that he had several panics during the therapist's absence.

Discussion at the conference focused on whether the therapist should mention these unreported panics to the patient. One participant in the conference viewed the behavior of the patient as an example of his being dishonest with the therapist, and believed that the patient should be confronted with this dishonesty, and that psychotherapy could not continue unless the therapist knew that the patient reported his perceptions as accurately as he could. A second person hypothesized that since the patient's accounting to the general physician (whom he had seen for one-and-a-half years) occurred during the therapist's absence, the panics were probably related to feeling abandoned by the therapist and that the report to the general physician was an attempt to secure an attachment.

The first discussant's argument seemed to be based on a general belief that honesty and completeness of information must be provided by the patient to the therapist, that the patient was exhibiting resistance, and that without trust, treatment will founder. The second discussant began to offer an individualized conceptualization of the patient: he had turned to the physician when feeling abandoned. We are also inclined toward this second interpretation.

There is little doubt that the patient was struggling with fears of loss of control. These fears of loss of control could be fears of being too aggressive or too sexual, since his panic was occasioned by loss of an aggressive lover. There was evidence, however, that his fears of loss of control had more to do with loss of connection and dissolution of ego boundaries, the patient's having referred to his panic in terms of death, dissolution, and identity loss.

We think that the patient, rather than lying or being dishonest, once he was reconnected to the therapist was in a different state, one in which he forgot his panics and which largely blotted out the other state. His "distractibility" then reflected these changes in state or identity shifts. In accordance with these state shifts was his description of rotating between living on junk food and taking up various health food fads, taking megadose vitamins, or going on diets to lose weight. He would buy food at the same healthfood store or eat the same menu ritualistically, and then shift to another system. When he started a diet, or started eating a particular kind of food or taking vitamins, he felt compelled to continue until the compulsion ran its course.

If we address the discrepancy in Mr. C's story as merely withholding of information, a kind of resistance which must be overcome, then dealing with it is easy. If we try to address who this person is and what the discrepancy means, then whether to confront him with the discrepancy at all or at this particular time, and how and with what end in mind, become relevant questions. These questions will be pursued next. How to handle such a discrepancy, what will work, and with whom and when depend on one's theory or therapy.

THE BASIC GOALS IN TREATMENT

Our goal in psychotherapy is to reduce the patient's pain and vulnerability to pain and to reduce his dysfunction and vulnerability to dysfunction. We try not to yield to any temptation to make the patient over according to an ideal of the "healthy" person. We try to design a treatment approach for a particular patient. We decide what is likely to work for that particular patient.

If the patient has a narcissistic personality and tends to experience attempts at giving him insight as narcissistic injuries, we doubt that offering insight is likely to be effective with him. If he experiences attempts at giving him insight as feeding and if a feeding relationship is experienced by him as curative, then we continue that approach. To any protest from psychoanalytically oriented therapists that patients should not be gratified, we respond, "Which patient?" and "To what end?" When a therapist objects to the patient's being gratified we may wonder if the therapist's goal is to make the patient into the therapist's ideal of a healthy person.

When an intervention results in a narcissistic injury, the patient generally makes a disturbance of some kind. It is less obvious to the therapist when an intervention, especially one directed toward insight, is experienced by the patient as feeding or narcissistic gratification. A patient may go through extended psychotherapy in which the therapist believes that insight through interpretation is the curative agent, but in reality the patient experiences the insights as his being given something. The experience of being given something makes the patient feel better and helps him to function better. It is not essential that a psychotherapist understand why a patient gets better except when something later goes wrong. Then, if the therapist understands what was working, he is in a better position to correct what is going wrong.

If we are right about Mr. C, of most importance to him were issues of attachment—being attached to, not cut off from, another human being—and of identity. Mr. C was subject to shifts in his identity, depending on his attachments and on his ability to structure boundaries by part functions.

Given this formulation, different approaches might be taken. Mr. C's discrepant accounts might offer an opportunity to work on his identity shifts. The therapist might have been justified in focusing on identity shifts, since if Mr. C were aware that he experienced parts of a whole as separate wholes, he might have been able to construct a corrective system. He might have been able to gain some measure of control over his cognitive processes and behavior, and over the intense feelings which are part of these processes. With control might come a *sense* of being more in control, which would enhance his self-esteem.

Following Masterson's (1976) lead, some therapists might try to make the patient aware of his clinging behavior and its destructiveness in relation to the issue of separation–individuation. The patient might then get in touch with his abandonment–depression and become able to recall earlier losses, such as the loss of his grandmother and the postulated (per Masterson) psychological abandonment by his mother, and to mourn those losses. It is conceivable that he could then gain awareness of the difference between his adult capacity and his helplessness as a child. The hope would then be that he would develop control over his response, not feel so helpless, and not have to cling.

If we thought these were achievable goals, we along with therapists more ambitious than ourselves[1] would still question such efforts directed toward insight at a time when Mr. C had been in therapy only 3 months and when the connection with the therapist was just developing. At this stage we would surely opt for repairing the connection damaged by the therapist's vacation. Bringing up the discrepancy between his reports to his physician and to his therapist could rupture the bond further. We favor restoring and maintaining the connection. Furthermore, we see the tie with the therapist as reparative for Mr. C.

What might our goals be for Mr. C, at this point in therapy and finally? In order to answer this, we need to consider some of his past coping techniques. First, we know he did things on his own. He was a self-taught mechanic. He had a certain talent that he developed through experience and action, not through study. Second, we also know he had a feeling for inanimate objects. When he drove from Michigan to Pennsylvania, he carried a spare engine in his car to make sure he could take care of himself and would never be stranded. He was self-reliant, nontrusting, and provident. He planned ahead in taking the extra engine. Similarly he made sure that he had enough money to cover his parking tickets so he could continue to park close to his safe places, thereby protecting himself from panic attacks. His safe places were at work, in his home, or in the car. Third, he also had the ability to divide or dilute attachments. He did not rely wholly either on his general physician or on his psychotherapist, and he had a group of friends rather than one significant relationship.

In addition to knowing Mr. C's coping tendencies, the therapist needs to understand what Mr. C wants from treatment and what his complaint means in order to determine a feasible goal for his treatment. When he presented his problem, it sounded as if he were hoping that the treatment would do away with his panic attacks and with his somatic problems. As he continued to tell his story, however, it sounded as if he might need something more. We view Mr. C's basic problem as a feeling of not being intact, of not having a sense of boundaries that hold by themselves. We postulate that he was trying to find a more comprehensive definition or definitions of self.

Most likely Mr. C would not give up his somatic concerns. His role as patient, seeing his physician regularly for minor complaints, was a defining role for him. He identified himself in part as "a medical patient." At the same time this role provided an attachment to the physician. A person such as Mr. C might have defined himself by attaching to a religion or a cause. Mr. C's brother and sister became followers of a Hindu guru, and we wondered if this might also be a solution for Mr. C. We question, however, whether he would have felt safe to put "all his eggs in one basket."

Mr. C seemed to feel safe only when he had contained himself within a physical boundary, such as his house or his car. In both circumstances his sense of safety resided in his being essentially alone in settings that provided boundaries and allowed him control over intrusions. We think the occupation of automobile mechanic gave him a greater sense of safety than his present occupation as a salesman, since his automechanic work allowed him more control over any intrusions and over his own mobility. He felt safe riding across the country in his car, with an extra engine, knowing that if his car broke down it was within his control to repair it. The ability to be mobile also served as a stimulus barrier for Mr. C, as did a container. The distractions he constantly experienced from intrusions when he was not alone in his house or in his car made him feel that he could not keep himself together. He could not keep himself focused because his attention was called to all the distractions at once, and he was buffeted about by each distraction. His hyperalert state was both his protection and his undoing. Unable to keep track of details, he forgot to put money in the meter and received parking tickets. He was unable to read because he felt he had to be alert to everything taking place around him. Because of his having to be constantly alert he could not work at anything that required his full attention. He felt safe when he thought he had provided for his own safety, e.g., by having enough money to pay the parking tickets so that he could park where he did not have to walk between his car and work, two islands of safety.

During the course of treatment, Mr. C took up computer training with the idea that he would have an occupation in addition to automechanics. It seems to us that this patient was more likely to choose solutions for his feeling of lack of intactness by developing multiple role identities, than to find a single comprehensive role, such as, husband, employee, or monk. In that way he would feel free to have "selves" that would "travel." Our aim would be to assist him toward this type of solution.

The original question—should we confront the patient with his inaccurate report—has become a very complex one that requires us to know who the patient is, his state and problems, his outside situation, the stage of the therapy, the methods to be employed, and the goals of the therapy. We are unable to answer, in a general sense, how a discrepancy is best addressed. In the case of Mr. C, given his need to diversify attachments and that he probably will continue to see his internist, and given the early stage of treatment, we would not confront him with this particular discrepancy.

Of course, this would also be in keeping with our notion of cure, which we will take up next.

"CURE"?

For psychological problems or illness it is not possible to think of cure without considering environment, especially social milieu. What we might consider aberrant behavior may be adaptive in a person's setting. For example, magical thinking is certainly adaptive in most cultures throughout the world. Somewhat self-centered delinquent behavior has true survival value in difficult times. Accordingly, it is presumptuous to define cure in terms of the proclaimed (probably not operative, certainly not usual) rules and customs of Western culture as we believe is often done by psychotherapists.

The tacit assumption of therapists that the goal of psychotherapy in all cases is *individual autonomy*, now often referred to as separation–individuation, creates a blind spot in understanding and helping certain types of patients. Ms. N, a 20-year-old, unemployed, white, single, practicing fundamentalist Protestant, high-school graduate from an urban, lower socioeconomic level family was discussed at a clinical teaching conference. She had been brought to the clinic by her mother on the recommendation of their family physician. Since the death of Ms. N's father a few months earlier, she had been several times to the family physician complaining of headaches, insomnia, and loss of appetite. Although Ms. N was herself uninterested in talking about what was on her mind, her physician told her it would be good for her to talk to someone at the psychiatric clinic. Shortly after her father's death, that same physician referred her mother to the clinic. Ms. N's mother was still being seen there for depression at the time of Ms. N's referral.

At Ms. N's first session her mother arrived with her and insisted on coming into the session. Ms. N's mother did most of the talking although the patient answered any questions directed to her. At one point the therapist gently suggested that the patient did not very much like to talk. Ms. N began to cry, whereupon her mother abruptly left the room. Ms. N explained to the therapist that this was also a hard time for her mother.

The therapist arranged the second session at the same hour that Ms. N's mother was seeing her own therapist so that Ms. N would have to come alone. She was more talkative and related better to the therapist in that session.

Ms. N canceled her third session, claiming her mother was ill. Neither she nor her mother appeared for any future appointments. Both therapists attempted to reach their respective patients, but the telephone had been disconnected, and letters netted no response.

The following history was obtained in the two sessions in which the therapist saw Ms. N. She was next to youngest of a sibship of six. She had one younger sister, two older brothers, and two older sisters. Both older sisters had children out of wedlock and were living with their children in the parental home along with Ms. N and her younger sister. It was unclear whether the brothers lived at home; they were in the house a great deal of the time. The patient stated that all of her sisters and brothers were different from herself in that they were "into sex and drugs." Her younger sister, whom she referred to as "fast," and her friends told Ms. N she would feel much better if she became sexually active. Her boyfriend, whom she had been seeing for about 1 year, was indeed interested in a sexual relationship but she believed he would leave if he "had his way" with her. She was considering the idea of trying to be more like her younger sister in 3 or 4 years if she were not married by that time.

Ms. N stated that around the age of 13 she realized that she was not like the other children in the family and that their behavior and values were not appealing to her. She stayed at home much more and became very devoted to her father. She actually followed him around the house and sometimes even went to his job with him and helped him. Upon inquiry the therapist learned that Ms. N and her father and mother were "very tight." This closeness increased over the 2-year period of her father's illness. Since her father's death, she and her mother had grown even closer. When she was unable to sleep at night she would go to her mother's room and she "knew" her mother would also be having trouble sleeping. They did not talk much about the loss of father, but merely spent that time together.

Ms. N spent her days watching television and did little else, except continuing to attend church regularly and to sing in the choir. Her father had been an elder in the church. Ms. N and her mother were the only other family members who attended church.

Ms. N told the therapist that she did not really feel that her father was gone: she still felt his presence in the house and in the church. She recounted an instance when she was looking for something in the dark and did not want to awaken her sister by turning on a light. The light went on, and she knew her father had turned it on for her. Another time as she and her mother were leaving for church, she saw a lamp shake and knew that father was expressing his wish that the other family members also attend church. She had never actually seen her father since he died, but he had appeared to other family members. She believed he was trying to appeal to them to mend their ways.

At the teaching conference discussion centered on whether Ms. N's mother should have been allowed to enter the first therapy session, what could have been done to help Ms. N to become autonomous, and whether what Ms. N was experiencing was a normal grief reaction. Ms. N had mentioned during the course of the second session that she would like to go to college, eventually have her own family, and get away from her mother's rule. She said that when one lived in her mother's house, one had to abide by her rules. When asked if her own rules would be different, her response was, "No. They would probably be the same rules."

Based on these statements most of the conference participants believed that the appropriate goal of treatment, had Ms. N continued, would have been separation–individuation, although this would have been a difficult task in view of the mother's stance, which was interpreted by most of the group as overprotective, controlling, and by a few even as symbiotic. Although the group recognized that it would have been difficult if not impossible to keep Ms. N's mother out of the first session, they generally agreed that a desirable objective would have been to keep the mother out of Ms. N's future sessions.

Some participants in the group considered the problems that would ensue if Ms. N were to become autonomous. One was the guilt she would probably experience upon leaving her mother. Another was that she would have to work through her grief in regard to the loss of her father before she could work through the guilt about leaving her mother.

The fact that the patient had left treatment, however, also had to be taken into account in discussing goals. We suggested that perhaps she was not capable of autonomy or perhaps autonomy is not relevant for her. It is possible that neither Ms. N nor her mother put the same value on individual autonomy as did the conference participants. The conference members' value system might obscure their understanding of the problem that Ms. N presented. Finally, we believe that an appropriate treatment goal could not be selected until we had a better understanding of the problem. The group did not agree with our admittedly controversial formulation, and insisted that autonomy is always preferable as it makes the individual less vulnerable to externals.

We propose that we might conceptualize Ms. N not as a separate individual but as part of a family constellation, of which her father was the center. The family, not the individual, was the unit that broke down, at least in the patient's and her mother's consciousness. This sense of a family unit was probably felt to some degree by the rest of the family as well. Within this family system each member had his role. While the patient designated herself, her father, and her mother as the core of the system, there were also other components, namely her sisters and their children, her brothers, and to some degree the church. With the father gone, there was no center to the system. However, the family defined the father as not really being gone. He was still functioning in his care-giving role when he turned on lights and in his role as family moralist, shaking lamps and appearing to the "fast sisters," pleading with family members to mend their ways. He was also present for Ms. N because of her close relationship with her mother and her connection with her father's church.

Although the system was damaged by the loss of its center, i.e., the father, it was beginning to mend through the family's denial of the father's death and through shifting alignments such as the increased closeness between

Ms. N and her mother. A likely explanation of the discontinuation of treatment by both Ms. N and her mother is that the therapist had communicated his intention to break the system apart. For Ms. N, the lack of an autonomous identity does not mean she will have no identity at all. Nor is she or the system in which she functions psychopathological merely because the system is not of value to the conference participants. In this case an intrinsic part of the system, the father, has shifted from being present in real life to being present in symbolic form. It appears to us that the forces that could bring this system back into equilibrium are already at work.

Although at the conference we did not focus on Ms. N's symptoms of depression, the question of how the depression should be treated still needs to be addressed. Assuming Ms. N is suffering from personal depression, rather than identifying with the depression of her grieving mother (an equally likely possibility), how would we approach treatment? If we conceive of Ms. N's depression as a normal grief reaction, would our aim be to help her grieve and give up her dead father? Our answer is, probably no. More consistent with our conceptualization of cure, i.e., what is likely to work, our aim would be to help strengthen and continue her connection with her father, in other words to support her denial of his death. Rather than help her give him up, we would help her feel comforted that he is still there as an enduring, although unseen, caregiver.

From our discussion of Ms. N, the reader can see that our notion of cure is relativistic, not absolute.

Chapter 3

STRUCTURALIST MODEL OF CHARACTER

CHARACTER STRUCTURE AND PERSONALITY

We have proposed that character structure is both a person's primary social investment, i.e., his life motive, and his style of processing social information (Malerstein & Ahern, 1982). Character structure is to us the most fundamental and abiding organization of a person as a social being. Personality[2]—obsessive–compulsive, hysterical, psychopathic, paranoid, schizoid, or narcissistic—was traditionally conceptualized in the psychiatric nosology as a relatively abiding clinical syndrome. Although character structure is not as apparent as personality, the two are alike in that both represent integrated clusters, not simply summations and accretions of characteristics. Character structure permits certain life investments to function with certain social cognitive styles but not with others. Similarly, one's personality welcomes certain traits or certain defenses but not others. For example, an obsessive–compulsive's tidiness goes well with punctuality, as both are served by the defenses intellectualization or undoing. A hysterical personality's flamboyance fits with an interest in getting affection, as well as with a preference for the defenses denial and manipulation. One personality type does not preclude another; being phobic or obsessive does not preclude being addictive or hysterical. Certain personality types, however, do tend to be linked together, such as obsessive and phobic. A person is less likely to be both obsessive and hysterical, although this combination occurs.

An individual's personality may be entwined with his character structure, his personality type expressing his primary investment and suiting his basic cognitive style. For example, the demand for precision that is a personality trait of the obsessive–compulsive suits the basic investment in function and in social codes, and the use of rigorous classification and gradedness that typify a particular character structure we call operational. In another individual, personality type, instead of being closely fit to character structure, is ancillary or superimposed upon it. The obsessive–compulsive trait that demands precision readily fits the rigorous logic that characterizes the operational's cognitive style, but may, in someone of different character structure, serve to cover a suspicious nature. Although the fit is more intimate and vital in one than in the other, in most individuals character structure and personality suit each other.

GENETIC EPISTEMOLOGY AND CONSTRUCTIVISM

Our theory of character structure formation synthesized our understanding of the psychodynamics of certain clinical syndromes and of Piaget's genetic epistemology (Malerstein & Ahern, 1982). Perhaps it is relevant here to explain Piaget's position as a constructivist. Interested in epistemology, Piaget turned to experimental psychology to study how the child develops knowledge; genetic epistemology is Piaget's own term for this process. Piaget belonged to the theoretical movement known as structuralism, in which the effort is to find and analyze the basic and abiding organized elements of a system. Within the broad structuralist context he may be classed as an interactionist and as a radical constructivist. As an interactionist he believed knowledge of reality is acquired through the knowing subject's interaction with the object to be known. As a radical constructivist he believed the child actively constructs his own world including knowledge of the self, Piaget being particularly careful not to invoke preformism or innatism of structures prematurely. As a radical constructivist, Piaget differed from fellow structuralist Chomsky, who argued that children's universal acquisition of complex articulated grammars implies that children have inborn linguistic structures (Piattelli-Palmarini, 1980). Piaget believed an innate tendency to autoregulation might explain not only universality of behavior but also any possibly innate language structures that might have evolved. He thought it likely that myelination of the neural tracts accounts for some of the stage changes in the sensorimotor period (birth to age two) (Piaget, 1981b). He clearly accepted the primitive reflexes, such as sucking and grasping, as inherited structures. Otherwise Piaget was inclined to ascribe development to the child's coordinating and equilibrating his interaction with the environment. Even a transformation in cognitive structure profound enough to be regarded as a major restructuring was viewed by Piaget as the result of equilibration of psychological structures. The radical constructivist view that all reality is a constructed reality and that the object of knowledge is actively constructed by the knower through interaction with the object contrasts with the more widely accepted view of reality, the Cartesian epistemology. In the Cartesian view, the knower and the known, the subject and the object, are separate givens. Psychotherapists influenced by the Cartesian view accept that the task of the individual is to get to know the objective and subjective properties of the world, thereby becoming more objective.

In constructivist epistemology, both subjective and objective properties are viewed as being actively constructed by the knower. This view does not deny "the existence of a reality external to the knower." It simply asserts that reality may only be known in terms of characteristics of the knower and, "more precisely, in terms of the modes of organization which the knower imposes on his experience" of his environment (Feffer, 1982, p. 11). In the constructivist view reality is reality *as known*. An infant, for example, knows (in the sense of know-how) an object as a function of his sucking activity, initially only in terms of his reflex schemes. Later he understands an object's length or width as he develops relevant cognitive structures to impose on his experiencing the object. Since objective reality, in order to be known, must conform to existing cognitive structures, the known properties are intrinsic to mental activity instead of being separate from it as in the prevailing Cartesian view (Feffer, 1982).

A psychological structure is a cognitive organization that may be inferred from observing an interaction. When a child sucks on objects Piaget (1962) inferred that he has a sucking scheme.[3] When a child repeatedly strikes an object and watches it swing, Piaget assumed the child has a striking-while-watching and watching-while-striking scheme, especially if he varies his striking or applies it to different objects. At the beginning of infancy these structures are primitive, centering around reflexes, although they include much more than that (see Malerstein, 1986, pp. 87–88). Later in the sensorimotor period and in the preoperational (ages 2 to 7), the concrete operational (ages 8 to 11), and the formal operational (ages 11 and on) periods the schemes or structures become more and more differentiated.

Piaget (1973) inferred that a child has constructed the structure of ordering, i.e., the structure of asymmetrical relationships, when he is able to arrange a set of objects according to size or according to depth of color. To be certain that the child has the mental structure for ordering it is expected that he show a plan; when ordering objects, he should not begin haphazardly but, for example, should start with the smallest or largest. He may also demonstrate that he has a structure for ordering by his grasp of issues that follow from understanding order, such as understanding transitivity (Piaget & Inhelder, 1969). That is, knowing A is greater than B, and B is greater than C, he figures out that A is greater than C without having to place A beside C.

Schemes or structures have the properties of repeatability and generalizability. If a child has a structure, he reapplies that structure again and again to the same event and object (repeating) and applies it to nonidentical, though similar, events and objects (generalizing). The infant not only sucks a particular block again and again but also sucks objects of different size, form, and texture. The older child may apply the structure of asymmetrical relationships when he establishes a hierarchy of objects in terms of depth of color as well as when he orders a series of uneven sticks according to size.

Before turning to our concept of character structure and character structure development, which deals with one's understanding of one's social world and of one's self as a social being, we note that Piaget (1965a, 1981a) theorized that developmental reorganizations of understanding of social objects were fundamentally no different from reorganizations of the understanding of physical objects. He proposed that development in the social and physical domains, if unimpeded, went hand in hand. Piaget (1981a) stressed that an object in every instance is affective as well as cognitive. Every object has a social component and affective valence, although depending on the particular object and one's experience with it, its social significance and affective valence may be small or large.

A chair is partly a social and affective object, not just a

physical object. At one extreme in a particular culture a chair may be a throne or an altar. Any cognitive construct of a chair in that culture includes some of the affective valence and social relationships of the throne or altar. Cognitive constructs of persons are likewise affective, but more so. Just as the affective components cannot be entirely split from the cognitive, so the social components cannot be entirely split from the physical component, and yet each is at least potentially distinct.

From the constructivist position that we construct our understanding of reality in terms of our cognitive structures, we assume that persons with similar experiences of the physical world construct a similar understanding of physical objects. Probably all of us would agree that an object with the configuration and substance of a chair is a chair. If we came from another culture, we might define that particular configuration and substance otherwise, e.g., as an altar or a thing at which to worship. Similarly with regard to a person as a thing or physical object, we would generally agree that someone is a girl or a boy, a blonde or a redhead. It is very unlikely, however, that we would all agree that a particular person is wise, kindly, or trustworthy. How social beings, including the self, and the social world are to be characterized socially is less universal. Although we all have much the same experiences of physical reality, our experiences of social reality are not the same. Therein is the starting point for our theory of character structure formation.

CONSTRUCTION OF CHARACTER STRUCTURE

We propose that character structure is constructed by a child (given his endowments) out of his experiencing of his social world (Malerstein & Ahern, 1982). He progressively builds his knowledge of his social world from his interactions with his social environment, particularly his interactions with his significant caregiver, usually his mother. If he experiences mother as a person who typically suits her own convenience and does not particularly meet his needs, he will come to see the social world as not concerned about others, and all persons as being "out for their own interests." He will understand the world as a place where it is best to look out for one's own interests; that is the way of the world and one must conform to it or lose out. Conversely if a child experiences his primary caregivers as having his best interests at heart, he will construct an understanding of the social world as one that cares about him. Those in authority will especially be thought of as invested in his best interests; he will believe he can look to them for assistance as needed. If a child is able to see some pattern to inconsistent caregiving, as from a mother who sometimes has his interests at heart but first focuses on the child's meeting certain interests of hers, he may be able to construct an understanding of others in which their interests have to be taken care of before they are more stable and may see to his. If a child experiences little pattern at all, he may not be able to construct an abiding internalized structure of what to expect of others or of himself. His view of social reality, of others, will be a shifting one, requiring frequent redefinition.

We think the form given to character structure draws heavily upon the two preoperational phases (ages 2 to 7) and upon the concrete operational period (ages 8 to 11). In the concrete operational period the child has the ability and tendency to coordinate attributes of objects, including not only thing attributes, such as height and width, but also social attributes, such as moral good and bad. The two basic components of character structure, primary social investment and social cognitive style, appear to be "set" in adults. Although it is not established when they become set, it was suggested (Malerstein, 1986) that a ma-

turational factor which induces reorganization in a succeeding developmental period or stage may limit access to
old styles of data handling, resulting in fixity of these earlier organizations. It would then follow that a similar maturational factor that induces formal operational thought
processing would close off and "set" styles of data processing developed prior to that time.

THE ROLE OF MATURATION

We hypothesize that major restructurings must be
triggered by some sort of organic shift and that maturational factors are critical in inducing change. Along with
this change comes a limiting or defining of access to old
ways of doing business. Piaget's position was not fixed
against such a possibility, but in the absence of proof of
maturational factors, he attempted purely psychological
explanations of the stage shifts. We fall into a particular
group of Piagetians, including Mounoud (1977) and Case
(1980), in emphasizing the role of the organic in inducing
developmental shifts. (It should be noted, though, that
the mechanisms we propose for inducing change and fix-
ing stages differ from those proposed by any other members of this group.)

We think that an organic restructuring is what ultimately makes possible the psychological structure of concrete operations, which is marked by the rigorous use of
classification and seriation when working with objects.
But we also think that if the interactions between environment and child are appropriate, then a preoperational
rather than concrete operational configuration will be the
psychological structure that abides. Our work (Malerstein
& Ahern, 1982) implies presence of a universal structure.
But we believe the universal structure to be a maturational
one, not the psychological structure of classification and

ordering. This universal structure allows for rigorous classification and ordering, i.e., for concrete operations, only if the child's experiences lend themselves to classification and ordering.

A major reorganization of mental structures, including character structure, begins around 7 or 8 years of age. This reorganization offers the child a knowhow that is adaptive to his immediate social milieu, his family, hence often to his subculture, thereby aiding his survival. Sometime after this, but before adulthood, character structure becomes firmly fixed (Malerstein & Ahern, 1982). The fixity of the structure allows social function in some measure to be relegated to automatic. Not having constantly to decide every response allows the older child and adult to relegate his more conscious responses to nuances.

One of the implications of a fixity of character structure is that change in psychotherapy is limited. We do not think that character structure is immutable, but a character structure type, once formed, may not be changed to another type. In formulating a plan for treatment of a particular patient we take character structure as a limiting parameter. We do not expect to replace the person's primary social investment or basic style of social cognition with a social investment or cognitive style belonging to a different character structure, although either social investment or cognitive style may be corrected for or modified in intensity.

NORMALITY AND CHARACTER STRUCTURE

Another implication of our theory of character structure development is that a child constructs his primary social investment and social cognitive style principally out of his experience with his significant caregiver and that since different children normally experience different kinds of caregiving, different kinds of normal character structure forms will be constructed.

Although we consider each of the different character structures to be normal, any character structure type may be pathological if the investment or cognitive style is exaggerated or if the defensive maneuvers for dealing with the character structure are exaggerated. Although it is true that one character structure type may have a more highly differentiated and coordinated cognitive structure and less primitive social investment than another type, we argue that level of differentiation is not a measure of normality *per se*. Whether one type of character structure is more normal than another depends greatly on what one defines as normal.

Ultimately, normality may be defined by species survival, hence by adaptability. If we define normality in cultural terms, then character structure type is relevant to the extent that a character type is adaptive to a particular culture or subculture at a particular time, survival in a particular culture and survival of that culture being derivative of the human animal's interaction with his world. If we were to define normal as average, then the more primitive character structure would be normal since it appears to be more frequent. In any case, we believe that primitive character is not bad; it merely more closely approximates the earlier developmental forms.

Pathology and normality are often defined by the culture that is in power. A society that relies on the mobility of the individual to explore new frontiers may prize autonomous functioning more than the close ties that characterize extended families. Protestants developed the premise that it was good to have an individual conscience, to be able to judge right from wrong, and to choose for one's self. Before that, European culture valued obedience and, at least in moral issues, obedience to the authority of the Catholic Church more highly than autonomy. Perhaps the recently popular dictum that only a therapist belonging to the same minority group as a particular patient can treat that patient arose from the experience of patients from different cultures with the value-trapped psychotherapists of our mainstream European culture. As long as clinicians continue to assume that character structure develops along a single continuum, that there is only one normal character structure, and that the more differentiated or coordinated character structure is the best, whether or not it is relevant to a particular patient or population, then such dissatisfaction will be justified. To the extent that psychotherapists deny the social reality their patients have constructed out of their own experience and its legitimacy, these clinicians will not "meet the patient where he is." In keeping with the cultural view that autonomy and the ability to choose are hallmarks of normalcy is the assumption by many Western psychotherapists that separation–individuation is desirable for everyone. This ignores the fact that most people in the world grow up in an extended family system in which identity as a member of a group is valued over identity as an individual.[4] More recently, with the advent of Kohut's work (1977), the opposite position has gained strength with some psychotherapy theoreticians. Some therapists assert that all persons need the constant, repeated validations of their undifferentiated self objects in order to feel whole and worthwhile (Baker & Baker, 1987). We disagree with this linear view as much as we disagree with the separation–individuation linear dimensional view.

A CONSTRUCTIVIST VERSUS A PSYCHODYNAMIC MODEL

Although our model utilizes psychodynamic understandings of clinical syndromes and in large measure owes its concepts to Freud and other psychoanalysts, particularly Abraham (1960), Bibring (1953), Bowlby (1969),

Deutsch (1942), A. Freud (1946), and Zetzel (1971), as well as Shapiro (1965), it differs from the psychoanalytic–psychodynamic model in several ways. First, we do not see character structure as developing along a single continuum with the most highly differentiated/coordinated character as healthy and the least differentiated/coordinated character as ill. This distinguishes our model from the usual psychodynamic model in which pathology and normality occur only on a single continuum of psychosexual development, ranging from dependency and undifferentiation to altruism and autonomy. As discussed in Chapter 2, our goal of treatment is not to help everyone become autonomous and altruistic, even if that were possible.

A second difference between our constructivist model and the psychoanalytic–psychodynamic model lies in the constructivist explanation of how children acquire knowledge of the world. According to Feffer (1982), psychoanalysis (along with other theories including behaviorism), buying into the Cartesian epistemology, assumes that, subject and object being separate, the subject's developmental task is to become more objective. Feffer proposed that any developmental theory must account for change and yet maintain continuity. Feffer pointed out that, in trying to account for change, Freud attributed to the child's mind adult characteristics, and when analyzing "the mind of the adult, he explained its psychodynamic properties by virtually equating it with the mind of the child," thus eliminating the difference between the two (Fischer & Pipp, 1982, p. 281). Feffer (1982) proposed that the constructionist (his word) point of view, in which subject and object are not separate, may offer a solution to the discontinuity–immutability problem encountered by Freudian theory. He promised a more complete presentation of a constructionist developmental theory (in his next work) and referred the reader to some earlier work (Feffer,

1967, 1970). From his presentations thus far he appears to deal with developmental change in the impersonal and interpersonal domains purely as a function of interaction and equilibrium. Certainly Feffer, by taking the constructionist–interactionist position, avoids the discontinuity between subject and object. In addition, he proposed that the organism confronted with an unfamiliar impersonal or interpersonal event, for which it has not already constructed appropriate hierarchical and integrated schemes, will take a *pars pro toto* approach in understanding that event. This conceptualization tends to avoid discontinuity between primary and secondary process. Feffer suggested that the organism, as an equilibrium seeker will later build a more adequate set of schemes, one that is hierarchical in organization. Feffer implied that he might be able to account for developmental change on this basis without discontinuity.

The concept of *pars pro toto* cognition as a nearly universal first approximation to a new experience has particular appeal to us and may partly explain problems we sometimes have with diagnosis. For example a patient we think of as having good reality testing may be a bit paranoid or may jump to an unwarranted conclusion when in an unfamiliar setting. Feffer's concept would not conflict with our proposal that there are some adults who display a distinctly high frequency of *pars pro toto* social reasoning.

It seems to us that a pure psychological system such as Feffer's, which posits a sort of cognitive conflict model, has difficulty accounting for discrete stages and periods. Such a system should develop almost evenly in all domains given the proper situations. While some stage shifts are a function only of interaction between self and object, as we have said (Malerstein & Ahern, 1982), we think others result from an interplay between maturation and the cognitive structures. Once a new maturational factor is in place, the cognitive structures exploit that factor, given interaction with appropriate aliment from the environment.

A major difference between the structural model and the psychodynamic or energic model is that (cognitive) structure, once built, does not require affect as a driving force. As important as affects and drives are in monitoring structures and as much as affects are a part of primitive structures, especially social structures, affects are not essential to activation of a structure or to its behavioral manifestations, once the structure is formed. Once a structure is developed, the structure tends to determine the form of activity taken whenever the psychological system is active.

Chapter 4

THREE CHARACTER TYPES

"We are all alike, but we are all different" (Sanford, 1948). As human beings we all share some things, and yet we are each unique. Between these two extremes lie many possible ways of grouping people, by religious beliefs, by language, even by body build. Our particular type of grouping, by character structure, is an important aid to choosing a rational approach to psychotherapy.

Style of social cognition, major life investment, and early caregiving experience distinguish each type of character structure from the other two (Malerstein & Ahern, 1982). A person of a particular character type has a distinctive style of social data processing. He has his own set of values or matters that are of most concern to him. Not surprisingly, he was raised in a particular way.

An isomorphism may be found between each of the three styles of social cognition in adults and a Piagetian period or phase of cognitive development: the operational period (ages 7 to 11), the intuitive phase (ages 4 to 7), and the symbolic phase (ages 2 to 4).[5] See Table 1 for a delineation of the qualities that distinguish each of our character types. In this chapter we swing back and forth between Piaget's ideas and our own. Those readers who do not know Piaget's work in detail may be uncertain as to which ideas are Piaget's and which are our own. We have tried in each instance to indicate which findings and concepts are Piagetian (as well as those of other authors). Where we fail to credit Piaget, we are most likely responsible for the position taken.

We adopted Piaget's designations—operational, intuitive, and symbolic—for our corresponding adult character types. Each character type approaches social life with a different kind of reasoning. When dealing with social matters, an operational character almost invariably employs operational social cognition, rigorously using classification and seriation of values when dealing with social objects. An intuitive character primarily uses intuitive social cognition. He values a social object according to a current aspect of its appearance, an attribute. Finally, a symbolic character regularly evidences transductive, symbolic, or preconceptual[6] social cognition. He defines a social object by an aspect of its appearance, by an attribute. He may confuse one object with another or an attribute with an object.

Basic social investment is a person's primary underlying motive, which guides his judgments and actions as a social being. This social investment is his major incentive, the principle goal that he repeatedly pursues and that is served by subgoals, although this may not be obvious to the person himself or to an observer.

Life investment is one of the three components we use to diagnose character type. This reigning investment sometimes may be heard in the theme(s) of the first interview. As the patient tells his story, we ask ourselves, "What does this patient want from me, from therapy, and from life?" One may hear an oral theme, a concentration on what the patient is getting or not getting. From another person, an attachment theme, an emphasis on loss, avoidance, or pursuit of attachment will emerge. From a third, an effort to function according to social convention or an effort to control function may be evident, including perhaps problems of initiation or inhibition of function. As to the patient's expectations from therapy or the therapist, some patients want narcissistic gratification; others want a friend, someone to be connected to, or a place to be; and others want self-understanding. Some want all three. This variety of expectations makes for a complicated system, but not an unbounded one (Malerstein & Ahern, 1982).

The second component important for character diagnosis is style of social cognition. Style of social cognition is a person's characteristic manner of processing social–emotional information, information about person relationships. Social cognition is distinguished here from physical cognition, i.e., cognition involving thing relationships, including cognition of person as thing, i.e., as a physical object. (Things may become social objects if a social system values them, e.g., diamonds or neighborhoods.) As we noted in Chapter 3, adults of the same culture tend to process their physical world similarly. They usually agree that an automobile is an automobile. Certainly not all adults of the same culture agree, however, on the composition of the social world. Some see it as a park, others as a jungle, and still others as a puzzling place to be.

These diverse views reflect our early experience in the world, particularly our experience with our parents. That experience is the third diagnostic component. In a sense we each see our social world as we believed it treated us. As we experienced life in our formative years, so we construct life and our part in it. Adults who early in life had different kinds of experiences with caregivers understand and process social and emotional data differently.

One group of adults conceptualizes values operationally. This group judges good or bad on the basis of abiding principles or rules: embarrassing someone is bad; giving to the poor is good; elders know better. Adults of another group typically base their value judgments on appearance: if it looks good, it is good; if it feels good, it is good. They reason from the end stage: they reason intuitively. A third group is concerned with whether an experience makes one feel whole or fragmented, attached or separate. Having a particular role in society or a sense of closeness to another person may both define and invest with value one's self and one's surroundings. According to this logic a similarity of appearance of two objects makes them the same object. Focus on a difference of appearance or form may cause the subject to view one object as two totally different objects. Accordingly class and subclass, degree and order, may be lost in this type of thought processing.

The social cognitive style of an adult patient may be distinguished by two parameters Piaget proposed to differentiate concrete operational cognition from preoperational cognition in children: classification and seriation (Inhelder & Piaget, 1969; Piaget, 1965b). Classification is the ability to understand class and subclass, the ability to include and exclude rigorously according to one or several attributes,[7] e.g., yellow versus green; yellow and green, but not yellow and black; or accident versus mistake. Seriation is the ability to understand the range, degree, or gradation of an attribute, e.g., depth of color, velocity, or seriousness of rule breaking. Ordinarily an adult precisely classifies or seriates in the physical domain, e.g., discriminating or grading colors. The adult may not, however, classify or seriate accurately in the social domain, e.g., he may not differentiate an accident from a mistake, or grade the seriousness of a transgression, depending on his emotional state and on who is involved.

THE OPERATIONAL CHARACTER

An operational character uses primarily operational social cognition. He draws lines between part and whole,

concrete and abstract, and intent and event. He coordinates different perspectives as he orders a hierarchy of
values and discriminates gradations; that is, he thinks in
degrees. From this we infer that in the social domain,
psychological structures or schemes of classification and
seriation exist for him and organize his social cognition in
familiar and unfamiliar social situations, i.e., the structures repeat and generalize. For example, if we think of
the construct of friendship, an operational knows that an
old friend who is abrupt with him during a phone call is
still his friend, that the friend may have been preoccupied
with something for the moment. The operational has an
understanding of conservation of friendship just as Piaget
(1965b) found a concrete operational child (age 7–11) to
understand conservation of matter. When lemonade is
poured from a short, wide glass into a narrow glass, the
concrete operational child understands that the amount of
lemonade does not change, even though it is higher in the
narrow glass and may look like more. A short time before
that period he might have insisted there was more lemonade in the narrow glass. Now he knows that although
the appearance changes, quantity is conserved. This is
parallel to understanding that an old friend is still an old
friend despite his behavior at a particular moment. An
adult who is an operational character has an autonomous
system of social values, a superego made up of abiding
goodnesses and badnesses. His codes are autonomous or
abstract in not being readily altered by the particular persons involved in an interaction, by current appearances,
or by affect. For example, stealing is bad whether it is easy
or difficult, and whether it is done by a Republican or a
Democrat, by himself or another. The operational's moral
classification is rigorous; thought and deed are distinct
from each other. An operational character grades social
value judgments much as a concrete operational child seriates quantity or length. An operational character does not
judge ill-mannered behavior as a major crime. Both a pre-

operational child and an adult of a different character type have more difficulty distinguishing minor from major infractions or transient from characteristic behavior (Piaget, 1965a).

There is a close tie between the type of judgment of values an operational character employs, i.e., his moral codes or conventions, and his investment in function in accordance with such values. Usually he is invested in the rituals and beliefs of his subculture as ends in themselves, whether the belief is in egalitarianism or aristocracy. It is not what he values but the stability or autonomy and gradedness of his values that distinguish his style of social cognition.

An operational character's anamnesis typically reveals that he experienced his caregivers as having had his best interests at heart, although perhaps as tending to be somewhat overprotective or controlling. It should be understood that, when we use the verb "experienced," we do so to stress what the child "made of" certain happenings, for example underprotection or overprotection. We do not assume some objective standard of underprotection or overprotection nor do we necessarily accept at face value the patient's words when he says he was under- or overprotected or that his caregiver was wonderful or dreadful. We attempt to reconstruct what he intuited from his interaction with his caregivers when he constructed his view of his social world.

A young woman's report that when she had a cosmetic reconstruction of her nose her mother did the same and that "Mother was just like a sister," leads us to reconstruct that the mother was perhaps narcissistic and competitive,[8] and not "out for her child's best interests." With a few more such data we then postulate that the patient experienced her mother as someone who also competed with her for "goodies" at a time when the patient's task was to construct her social world, and herself as a social being. To that patient the social world looks out for itself. "It's human nature. It's the way things work," she will contend.

Unlike the mother of the above-mentioned patient, an operational's mother is experienced as "out for her child's best interests." Overemphasis by the parent or misinterpretation by the child of this protective style of caregiving may readily be experienced as overprotective or controlling. The child's construct of others, particularly those in authority, will then include their wanting to overprotect or to control him. Thus, issues of who is in charge of his function, himself or the authority figure, are often of special concern to an operational character. It is also no surprise that obsessive–compulsive traits, traits which involve control, are often part of an operational character's makeup.

Piaget (1973) showed that in the concrete operational period a child is able to understand attributes and values of objects as abstract entities and as existing in degree. That is, the concrete operational child understands attributes such as amount, redness, or heaviness as being separate from any particular object. (The child may not use adult terminology in speaking of such an attribute, only being able to address quantity in terms of, for example, "more sweets to eat.") He has knowhow in dealing with attributes. He can order a series of sticks according to size. He can also sort according to multiple, i.e., combined, attributes, e.g., shape and color, as in culling red squares from blue squares, blue disks, and red disks. (A younger child in the process of culling red squares may at some point start to cull red disks as well.)

Similarly, with regard to moral values, the concrete operational child understands honesty and dishonesty both in quantitative and in qualitative terms. He is not likely to suggest a severe punishment for a minor transgression (Piaget, 1965a). He distinguishes a lie from a mistake. Lying, as an attribute, is a coordination of the inaccuracy of one's story with the intent one has, a multiplicative class like blue squares. Moral values are autonomous to the concrete operational child. For example, stealing is stealing whether or not the perpetrator is caught and whether he is taking something from an adult or from a peer (Piaget, 1965a). This is not so to the younger child. The younger child might regard taking something from a peer as not stealing, whereas taking something from an adult would be stealing. If something bad happens to a person, a younger child assumes that the person has done something wrong. Similarly, if a person is not punished, the younger child may judge that person's actions as correct.

Inherent in the concrete-operational-stage child's understanding of attributes or values is coordination of superficial discrepancies. A ball of clay, i.e., make-believe candy, when elongated into the shape of a candy roll does not fool a concrete operational child into thinking he has more "candy" to eat. He knows he still has the same amount despite its current appearance (Inhelder, Sinclair, & Bovet, 1974). A younger child may insist an elongated piece of "candy" is more to eat. A concrete operational child understands that if he says he saw a dog as big as a cow, this is not a greater lie than saying he received a C in a course when he received a D (Piaget, 1965a). A younger child in his judgment of right and wrong is influenced by the degree of exaggeration. He reasons that passing the course is possible; hence saying that he passed is not as wrong as saying he saw a dog as big as a cow. The concrete operational child no longer judges the moral wrong in lying by the size of exaggeration.

We propose that a concrete operational child may be expected to have the capacity to judge whether the grownups with whom he lives look out for him or not (Malerstein & Ahern, 1982). For such a judgment, we would expect certain attributes of persons to be coordinated, e.g., words and deeds. Specifically, does this person keep his promises or not? Do his words match his deeds? If he agrees to take me out for a treat later, does he do so? Is he reliable? Will he be out for me in the long run, even though I have to forgo pleasure now and even though he does not appear to be out for me in the short run? Abstractions such as controlling, overcontrolling, and undercontrolling; protectiveness, overprotectiveness, and underprotectiveness; and trustworthiness and nontrustworthiness are attributes that coordinate superficially discrepant parameters. The child is asked to restrain himself, something he finds unpleasant, in order to please this same person who gives him a promised treat later. The child when he is slow in a dangerous situation may be punished or hurried by the same person who praises and encourages him when he is slow to learn to feed himself, tie his shoes, or do his ABCs. He may be shouted at when he intentionally causes damage and comforted by the same person when he causes damage by mistake. In the concrete operational period a child can recognize that a person who at times causes him pain is still on his side. The same kind of coordination of surface discrepant parameters is involved when a father jokes pleasantly with a child and appears friendly, but keeps few promises and uses the child's or family's money for himself. This child will comprehend his social world as nontrustworthy and not out for him in the long run. We will discuss this child and his world when we discuss the intuitive character.

Piaget (1965a) found that children in the concrete operational period distinguished mistakes from purposeful acts. We propose that understanding the abiding attribute of a caregiver's being in one's corner, which requires one to ignore temporary hurts, is no different in form from assessing whether an act is mistaken or purposeful, which also requires one to ignore the damage caused. A seven-

or eight-year-old can distinguish a lie from a mistake (Piaget, 1965a). He knows that a small child who says 2 + 2 = 5, or a child who does not know the names of the streets in his town and thus misleads someone, is making a mistake, not lying. To a younger child, a lie and a mistake are the same, and the blame justified by the act depends on the resulting damage. Initially, a child thinks that telling lies is wrong because one will be punished. He also thinks that it is naughtier to tell a lie to an adult because one will be caught. Later, a lie is thought to be bad even when it is successful. The older child may point out that "if everyone lied no one would know where they were" (Piaget, 1965a, p. 171).

A child as young as 6 years old (though usually somewhat older) may understand that if a child's intentions are good when he acts, any damage caused may be discounted (Piaget, 1965a). Piaget asked children if a child who tries to fill daddy's empty ink well in order to help daddy but then spills some ink and causes a stain is naughtier than a child who knocks over daddy's ink well when playing. Concrete operational children are able to discount the amount of damage, e.g., the size of ink stain, and take intentions into account.

The basic coordination in understanding truthfulness (lies versus mistakes) or trustworthiness (trying to help someone but sometimes faltering or sometimes causing short-term pain) does not differ from the coordination involved in understanding conservation of matter (Malerstein & Ahern, 1982). Admittedly, however, constructs in the social sphere are more difficult than those in the physical sphere, because both the caregiver's and the child's emotional states and the child's ability to perceive social–emotional data fluctuate more than do size or color of a particular physical object, or the ability to see, feel, or label physical objects (including persons as physical objects). We (Malerstein & Ahern, 1982) postulated that an operational character as a child coordinated these seemingly contradictory messages, such as being waited for under some conditions and prodded under others, into his understanding of the type of caregiving he received. During the concrete operational period the child can coordinate these surface contradictions into a sense that his parents and his social world are to be trusted, that they look out for him, that they are invested in his best interests. We proposed that he is able to coordinate into his view of his mother her saying such things as "Be quiet, or I will spank you" or "Be quiet, and I will take you out for an ice cream." Since she is generally consistent in what she says and does, he constructs, in spite of his mother's being bad to him some of the time, a view that his/the social world is basically good to him, that his social world is basically to be trusted, that his mother means what she says, that her promises or words are kept, that promises are to be relied upon, and that if he goes along with others, things by and large work okay. As we shall see in the next section, given different aliment, such as failure to carry through on promises, the future intuitive character constructs a radically different understanding of his mother and his social world.

The adult operational's construct is that the social world may be trusted, that others, particularly those in authority like his primary caregivers, will say what they mean and mean what they say, and that they have his best interests at heart. Even when from time to time he finds this is not the case, he still operates on this assumption, although this causes him difficulty or disappointment. The fact that the assumption repeats itself and generalizes to people other than his parents implies that a cognitive structure of trust in others exists for the operational character. Conceiving of and trusting in a future, he is able to postpone gratification. His superego is autonomous, made up of principles: lying is bad; intentions behind an action are often as important as results; promises are to be kept in spite of delays or discomfort. Since his moral judgment of himself rests on such internal criteria, his self-esteem is not overly vulnerable to external circumstance or to strong affect. If things go wrong, or if he is in pain, he does not assume that he did something wrong or that he was a bad person. This is in contrast to an intuitive character who, like an intuitive-phase child, might assume he is bad because he finds himself in bad or painful circumstances.

THE INTUITIVE CHARACTER

The style of social cognition of the intuitive character is the inverse of the social cognitive style of the operational character. Whereas the operational character judges on the basis of abiding principles, e.g., being truthful is good, the intuitive character typically judges on the basis of appearance: "If it looks good, it is good," "If it feels good, it is good," "If it feels bad, it is bad," and so on. He reasons from the most striking current aspect. He reasons backwards from the end stage, i.e., from a conclusion.

An intuitive character may note a current quality of a person and reason: "He is nice to me, so he must be a good person." An intuitive regularly ignores his previous experience, e.g., that this person was nice to him in the past in order to get something from him or that the person who appears to be treating him well at this moment disappointed him in the past. Typically he fails to coordinate such a multiplicatory class of superficially contradictory behaviors, just as the intuitive phase child is unable to deal with a multiplicative class (Inhelder & Piaget, 1969) such as blue squares (made up of both blueness and squareness). For the intuitive character badness or goodness, friendliness or competitiveness, and trustworthiness or untrustworthiness as attributes are not separable from momentary behavior. Anyone who is caught and punished, including himself, must be bad or guilty and if one is not caught, he must not be bad. His social thought processing is intuitive. His superego (actually a superego precursor), i.e., his system of values, is not autonomous. For the intuitive, what is good for him and/or good for the moment is good generally.

Ms. S told her therapist that the man with whom she was having an affair wanted to end the relationship because he felt guilty about cheating on his wife. Ms. S didn't feel guilty about cheating on her husband because as she explained she was enjoying the affair and getting so much out of the relationship that there could not be anything wrong with it. "If it feels good, it must be good." Such rationalizing or justifying is generally considered to be a defense. In our model, if Ms. S's judgments are generally made using such end-stage reasoning, i.e., rationalization, they reflect the intuitive style of cognition. Intuitive cognition is influenced by whichever attribute is in focus—the one which is most striking at the moment. Ms. S focused on how the relationship made her feel. She judged the moral value of her affair on that basis alone.

An intuitive character is as certain of his logic as the operational is of his own. And in much of the world, including the microworld the intuitive was raised in, it is the logic that works. Just as an intuitive-phase (5 to 7 years) child is fully convinced that the car which arrives first is the fastest car (Piaget, 1954), Ms. S fully embraced her reasoning that anything that feels good is moral. She could acknowledge that determining right only by what makes each person feel good at any given time in effect eliminates social standards, and could understand this viewpoint when it was discussed apart from her own interests (as a kind of formal operational exercise). When faced with an action to be taken, however, she employed her preoperational logic and argued her case well.

Ms. S's basic, automatic style of social cognition has the same form as the social and physical cognition of the child in the intuitive phase of the preoperational period. The child in the intuitive phase does not understand values or attributes of objects or events, including moral values, as abstractions separate from immediate experience (Piaget, 1965a). A 5- to 7-year-old is limited to a single perspective: his own immediate perspective. He does not integrate past or other perspectives or variables into abiding attributes and values. He does not realize that certain attributes of an object remain constant even though that object is transformed in appearance.

Ms. S, reasoning on the basis of the most striking attribute, her current affect, demonstrates that she lacks a structure of conservation for conventions or moral codes. Someone else might have said, "I know it is cheating and cheating is wrong. But I'm going to do it anyway," or might have believed that infidelity is not immoral for women, or that it is also fine for husbands to have affairs. As noted, the moral code or convention is not the issue. The identifying features are the lack of autonomy of the value or code and the type of reasoning employed.

Typical of the intuitive-phase child's and the intuitive character's thinking is their difficulty in seeing a situation from another person's point of view. An intuitive-phase child, looking at a model of three mountains, will assert that were he or another child to look at the model from a different vantage point the view would be the same view he now has (Piaget, 1937). This egocentric perspective is also heard in Ms. S's response to her boyfriend's request that she try to look at things in terms of "where he is coming from." She replied that he should look at things in terms of where she is coming from. When her therapist suggested that perhaps she "might be more persuasive" if

she could understand her boyfriend's viewpoint, she
agreed with this suggestion and for a time made an effort
to do so, but eventually slipped back into her egocentric
position.[9]

Intuitive thinkers have trouble with seriation, with
thinking in degree. If intuitive phase children are asked to
order sticks of different length, they order two or three
correctly, but not an entire series. They may arrange the
sticks like an ascending staircase, but the baseline will be
jagged (Piaget, 1965b). Adult intuitive characters have difficulty thinking in degree in the social sphere. If they perceive themselves or another person as having a flaw, they
judge themselves or that person extremely harshly. Intuitive characters tend to judge in terms of absolutes of right
and wrong, just as the intuitive-phase child sees the rules
of the game of marbles as being absolute: such children
when playing marbles claimed that the rules were made in
heaven and allowed no deviation (Piaget, 1965a). Being
once disappointed by another person may be grounds for
the intuitive adult to discard that person. Similarly, although an intuitive character is usually successful in projecting blame outside himself, when he does accept blame
he may see himself as rotten.

Both the intuitive-phase child and the adult intuitive
character believe in immanent justice: "You get what you
deserve and you deserve what you get." Piaget (1965a)
tested children by telling them stories such as one about
boys who stole apples and then crossed a bridge that col-
lapsed under them. When asked why the boys fell in the
water, an intuitive-phase child typically responded, "Because they stole the apples." Kohlberg's (1963) similar
studies showed that preoperational children judged a
child as good if he received a reward. If something bad
happens to one, one must be a bad person. If something
good happens to one, one must be good. If what Ms. S did
felt good, then what she did must be good and she must

be a good person. (This concept is in keeping with the Calvinist teaching that if one is prosperous, God is rewarding one for being good, and if one is poor, one is being punished for being bad.) An intuitive character's system of moral values, i.e., his valuation of self and others, in large measure comes from outside, from narcissistic supplies, adulation, riches, excitement (or their opposites). The intuitive character has a heteronomous superego rather than an autonomous superego. Without an autonomous system of values, he depends on external clues or how he feels at the moment, and what he is getting or has, to measure goodness and badness.

An intuitive character's style of social cognition, i.e., his way of judging on the basis of current appearances or externals, is entwined with his investment in narcissistic supplies, i.e., in getting and having. Basically, an intuitive character wants what makes him feel good now. Since how he feels, including how he feels about himself, depends on externals, on what is happening to him at the moment, his self-esteem may be subject to considerable momentary flux. When something bad happens to an intuitive character, reasoning from the endstage he may momentarily feel that he must have deserved it. However, by externalizing, denying, and projecting, intuitive characters rapidly defend their self-esteem most of the time.

The intuitive character's experience of early care was different from that of the operational character. Generally, as an intuitive describes his early caregivers, the therapist will note that the caregivers were absent, changing, or unavailable, or available as suited their own convenience (narcissistic), or at least not particularly invested in their child's best interests. If primary caregivers were unavailable through death, divorce, or illness, the child was left to look out for himself. Available caregivers who were primarily concerned with their own interests could be expected to scold the child when they were inconvenienced and to praise him when he did something they enjoyed. In such a relationship promises could not be counted upon, because "making good" on a promise might not suit the caregivers' convenience when the time came. The future intuitive thus determines that he may rely only on what he is getting at the moment. Delay of present pleasure is pointless, and only what is before him matters. To the intuitive there is only one variable—his current gratification or nongratification. He does not construct superordinate principles in order to weigh future reward against present pleasure. Learning early that he is largely on his own in terms of looking out for his own interests,[10] he may at worst be impulsive and untrustworthy, manipulative, and even predatory.

On the other hand, the intuitive character is also the character type best able to capture the moment, to seize an opportunity, and to put a little joy in the day. Putting a good face on things, he may be diplomatic and charming. He may lend smoothness to the interfaces between individuals and groups. The intuitive character usually assumes that others, like his caregivers, are not trustworthy. Generally, he does not believe the promises of others. What counts is action. Management, business, competitive sports, entertainment, and international affairs cannot do without him.

THE SYMBOLIC CHARACTER

The symbolic character structure is more complicated than either the operational or the intuitive character structure. Whereas the latter two are pure types, among symbolic characters there are pure symbolics and subtypes. The subtypes have an operational and/or intuitive cast to their symbolic structure. Regardless of subtype, however, all symbolics share a characteristic style of social cognition, basic investment, and experience of early care. Although an operational symbolic may be precise as an operational is in coordinating the dimensions of attributes, that precision generally serves the symbolic's requirement for self and object definition. Similarly, an intuitive symbolic fits certain intuitive traits into the cognition and investment of a symbolic; for example, pursuit of acclaim may help to define the symbolic or to connect him to another.

The customary social cognitive style of patients we classify as symbolic characters is preconceptual. In preconceptual cognition a representative of a class is not distinguished from the class itself. One robin makes a spring and spring guarantees robins. Having had a bad relationship with a woman, a symbolic may abandon all relationships with women. Having had a poor treatment experience with one therapist at a facility, he may reject that facility and all similar ones. One woman asserted she understood perfectly all alcoholics and all spouses of alcoholics because she was married to an alcoholic. There is a diffusion of boundaries between the attribute of an object, part object or symbol, and the object itself. Wanting to be like the young men who were burning their draft cards, one young man destroyed his welfare card. Upon experiencing a financial setback the preconceptual thinker may view himself as a poor person; when he has a financial success the next day he may view himself as a rich person. Whatever part of reality is in focus becomes the whole reality. Words, wishes, fantasies, facts, and deeds may in some measure be interchangeable. Those who think preconceptually may act on the basis of any of the above as though they were all real. Basically, preconceptual thinking does not distinguish part object or attribute from whole object, and hence, one object from another.

A social agency administrator who could argue thing-issues—issues involving furniture, financial investments, staffing ratios, even higher mathematics and theoretical physics—with flawless logic ran his agency preconceptually. When he received a complaint about poor delivery of service, he immediately made new policy that pacified the complainer. Chaos resulted as he failed to foresee that the policy change would have many more effects on the system than the mere accommodation of the complainer. He saw the part—the single complaint—as representing the whole, poor delivery of service. Another administrator, having the idea that her agency needed "new blood," set up a system for evaluating everyone, including current employees along with new applicants. She planned to rid herself of ineffective employees and get new, better-qualified workers. It did not occur to her that the current employees would dislike this plan, much less that they would be angry enough to go to the governing board. Like the blind men feeling a part of an elephant, she addressed only one part without considering the whole.

Children in the symbolic or preconceptual phase of cognitive development do not differentiate attributes from objects, and hence do not fully differentiate one object from another (Piaget, 1962). They do not make use of classes and subclasses of objects. Piaget's daughter, almost 3 years old, reasoned that a dog that was gray was a cat because the cat she knew was gray. A preconceptual child uses transductive or particle-to-particle reasoning. She takes the part, e.g., the attribute of grayness, for the whole identity of the object—the cat.

The child's preconceptual reasoning is not different in structure from that of an adult halfway house manager who used patients' employment status as the measure of successful treatment. To this woman, any patient who got a job and could move out of the halfway house was successfully treated. The manager did not take into account a patient's being miserable or suicidal when living alone and employed. She saw the parts, the two attributes of getting a job and living out of a communal setting, as the whole of "successful" treatment. She took representatives of a class, one or two possible measures of successful treatment, as the class of successful treatment itself.

It is important to note that preconceptual social cognition has advantages. This same manager's single-minded style of pursuit was the force without which this much-needed community resource would not have been established. Her halfway house continued long after she left.

For a symbolic-phase child, if an attribute of an object changes, then the object becomes a different object (Piaget, 1962). Piaget's (1962) daughter, Jacqueline (age 2½), seeing her sister, Lucienne, in a bathing suit and cap thought her a different person from the Lucienne whom she was accustomed to seeing in a dress. Jacqueline understood the object, Lucienne, to be a different object because her costume, a part object or attribute, had changed. An adult patient who exhibited similar confusion saw the therapist as a friend in one session, as an untrustworthy person in the next session, and in a third session as a pitiful person requiring the patient's help. This symbolic character saw the therapist as being whatever attribute the patient perceived at the time. Such a patient does not sense the therapist as an abiding whole person with varying attributes. His psychological structures for formulating concepts of social/emotional matters, matters such as trust–distrust, generous–stingy, kind–mean, loving–hating, are undifferentiated from his construct of the object.

A symbolic/preconceptual-phase child confuses a symbol of his activity, a part object or attribute, with his identity. If he puts on a sheriff's badge, he becomes the sheriff (Maier, 1965); if she scribbles with a pen on paper, she is a writer (Millar, 1968).

Considering the direction of development from undifferentiated to differentiated, we would expect that at this stage the child fails to distinguish the real from the imaginary. We assume that in some instances a child may mistake the real thing for make-believe. Adults are struck by how seriously children may take make-believe. This is much like our observation of a schizophrenic when we note his concreteness when an abstract communication is intended, but fail to note his abstractness when the intended communication is concrete. The point is that abstract and concrete are not clearly separate from each other. The child equates identity of the self as an object with a symbol. We see adult symbolic characters who also confuse identity with a symbol of an activity. Some define themselves by a single activity or a combination of activities or in terms of one social role, such as parent, artist, or therapist.

Preconceptual children reason on the basis of contiguity or similarity (Piaget, 1960, 1962). Objects and events that occur together are assumed to be associated. One may be assumed to cause the other. Turning the steering wheel makes the car go; mist and clouds are related to daddy's pipe smoke. Young children connect everything to everything else. (We think they fail to disconnect one thing from another, since as we just noted initially everything is undifferentiated from everything else.)

Symbolic characters do the same: "As I was thinking about an accident, an accident happened." "She was late for her therapy on Friday. So she *must* be resisting therapy." This overconnecting of experiences, on the part of both symbolic-phase children and adult symbolic characters, makes a kind of sense out of happenings. It offers a kind of understanding of what is going on around them, a kind of knowing. It makes things familiar; it incorporates whatever happens into what is known. Connecting is the essence of thought processes; Piaget calls this assimilation. If the primary mode of operation is to assimilate, to connect everything to everything else, then this will be the nature of the unimpeded system.[11]

The preconceptual cognition of the symbolic-phase child does not fully differentiate objects and events from values and attributes. Since essentially an attribute is a part object, a symbolic child regularly fails to distinguish part object from whole object, including part self from whole self. The symbolic-phase child and the adult symbolic character, for whom attribute or part object is undifferentiated from whole object, do not appropriately recognize the essence of the object or of the self. Hence both the 2- to-4-year-old child and the symbolic adult blur the boundaries between objects, including the boundary between the self and another object.

Integral to the preconceptual style of social cognition and confusion about identity is the symbolic character's investment in regulating attachment. This investment in attachment may be manifest not only by desire for and pursuit of attachment but also by its opposite—avoidance of attachment. Regulation of attachment will affect identity and intactness of identity. In one symbolic the need may be to attach to someone or something outside the self in order to feel whole. In another symbolic the need may be to exist sufficiently separate from others, so as not to merge, not to lose all sense of self. When unattached, symbolic characters may feel they have no identity, no center; they may feel lost, "cut off," "in between," "incomplete," and "like a ship without a rudder." Although some symbolic characters tend toward attachment and merger in order to feel whole, they at the same time may be afraid of such attachment or merger, recognizing that it may result in identity confusion or vulnerability to pain attendant on separation and loss should the relationship not last. Either striving toward merger or avoiding merger is the essence of the investment in attachment.

A symbolic character having problems with identity, i.e., with knowing who he is and finding his direction or goals, may depend on external clues. While the intuitive is unable to know his value as separate from externals, the symbolic has not constructed a knowledge of himself as a social entity separate from externals. A symbolic character may center himself around some other person to define himself, mirroring the activities or concepts of the loved one. Sometimes deep involvement with a cause or social movement helps a symbolic to feel whole. Some symbolic characters diversify their attachments, making multiple attachments to insure some degree against loss.

Many symbolics, in keeping with a lack of definition and a need to overconnect, may have little stimulus barrier. Everything is incorporated into their systems. Such persons are overly sensitive to vagaries of external input, e.g., whether they succeed or fail in an endeavor or whether they are liked or disliked, with accordant global shifts in self and object concept including value of self and object, e.g., sense of omnipotence or hopelessness. Focused on an imposition, such a symbolic may feel usurped and be overcome with humiliation and rage. Accompanying this cognitive unboundedness, affect—love, rage, depression, or panic—may be diffuse and overwhelming.

Since a symbolic character may not clearly differentiate a part from the whole, an attribute of an object from the object itself, he may also relate to a part of himself as though it were his whole self. He may, for example, define himself in terms of some social role and see that role as his identity: a career employee, a student, a therapist, a recovering alcoholic, or a father. He is at once attached to and defined by the role. If the attachment to the role is broken, his sense of significance may be lost, and he may not know how to define himself and may feel incomplete or fragmented. Most symbolic characters do not actually fragment, in the sense that they do not hallucinate, become delusional, or have loose associations.

We maintain that most symbolic characters have satisfying attachments and that these symbolic characters probably constitute the majority of the normal population. Depending on their coping mechanisms, most symbolic characters remain in an integrated state when they feel connected with someone or with some activity, cause, or role, or combination of these. When the connection breaks, however, they may feel fragmented. When they are connected again, they once more feel integrated. We do not often see people who have satisfactory attachments in our office as patients.

We have been studying transcripts of interviews of normal subjects. Preliminary findings suggest that two investigators, each blind to the other's findings, reliably assign adults and adolescents to one of our three character types.

One of the incidental findings of the study was that a significant proportion of the symbolic characters not only had good attachments but also had relatively stable, though troubled, identities. We recognized, for example, baby identities, narcissistic identities, identities as treater or even as the treatment (for an ill mother),[12] and as the perfect mother. These identities create their own problems, although they offer some sense of stability in establishing a feeling that one knows who one is and where one is going. Yet these subjects, who have near-adequate identity solutions, display the investment in identity and attachment issues and the characteristic social cognition and caretaking history which are earmarks of the symbolic character.

Subtypes of Symbolic Character

Earlier in this chapter we described the child's experience with his caregivers, from which he constructs either an operational or intuitive character structure. The operational experienced his caregivers as largely placing his interests first. The intuitive experienced his caregivers as not sufficiently available or as out for their own interests. We reconstruct that symbolic characters experienced their caregivers as requiring that certain interests of theirs (the parents) be met first by their child before they as caregivers can see to the interests of their child or be more predictable. This results in the child having less separation of himself from caregivers, i.e., his social world, and being less distinct in his definition of his self. A caregiver who needs to be overprotective disregards the child's needs to some degree. The child is serving the caregiver's need. If this factor is pronounced the child may be expected to become a symbolic.[13] But to the extent that this overprotectiveness serves the child's needs, he may be operational, his symbolic character structure has an operational cast, and we call him an operational symbolic. To the extent that a caregiver may be seen continually to consider herself before she becomes a satisfactory caregiver for the child, that child will construct an intuitive cast for his symbolic character and will become an intuitive symbolic. We also see mixed symbolics with both operational and intuitive characteristics who presumably experienced their caregivers as both protective and nonprotective and as requiring that the child meet certain of their emotional needs before they meet the child's needs.

Since we have now defined our conceptualization of the three character types and the symbolic subtypes, we will make a few additional comments regarding structure which we did not make in Chapter 3. These involve our concept of the social-ego.

THE SOCIAL-EGO

In contrast to the tripartite structure of psychoanalysis—the superego, ego, and id—our structural system implies a bipartite structure—the social-ego and physical-ego.

The social-ego deals with self, other persons, and even nonliving things in so far as these things are accorded social value, e.g., diamonds or houses in prestigious neighborhoods. The physical-ego deals with nonliving things but also with persons, including the self, as things, in so far as they do not carry social value. We view the social-ego as distinct from the physical-ego because we find persons who readily use formal operational reasoning when dealing with things and who regularly have preconceptual or intuitive components of reasoning when dealing with social objects. The cognitive schemes of the social-ego are more affectively laden than those of the physical-ego.[14] The social-ego consists of conventions and morals, e.g., manners, the difference between the two being merely quantitative (Malerstein & Ahern, 1982). Since we see no qualitative separation of conventions and morals, we make no clear demarcation between superego and ego.

In our concept of character structure are postulated demarcations within the social-ego. Each of the different character structures is marked by a different type of undifferentiation in the social-ego. In the operational, any undifferentiation between self- and object representation is in terms of function. Basically, he has a autonomous social-ego. His typical question is, does he own his function as a social being or does his parent, wife, or boss?

For the intuitive, undifferentiation in the social-ego is in terms of valuation. His social-ego is heteronomous. If he is loved, he is good. There is also a kind of differentiation of social-ego from physical-ego in terms of values; for example, an intuitive may feel he is a valuable person because he has a valuable home. If he has a valued (good) thing, he is a valued (good) person.

In the symbolic's social-ego we find an undifferentia-

Table 1. Character Structure

Character type	Historical experience	Overriding investment	Fundamental social cognitive style	Arena of undifferentiation	Types of social ego
Operational	Caregiver looked out for my best interests	Function and control of function	Operational (concrete) (age 8–11)	Function or who is in charge	Autonomous
Intuitive	Caregiver looked out for caregiver's own interests	Getting and having	Intuitive (age 5–7)	Valuation of self and others	Heteronomous
Symbolic	Caregiver looked out for my best interests or was more predictable, provided caregiver made to feel whole and worthwhile	Identity and attachment	Symbolic (age 2–4)	Identity of self and objects	Autonomous to heteronomous, or a mix of the two.

tion between self and object, one object and another, and part object and whole object, as described above.

We think there is a social-ego formation somewhat separate from physical-ego formation, each monitored by affective activity and both potentially connected by values (or by defensive operations that attempt to invalidate or hide the connection or value). As already indicated, we think the systems constructed during the concrete operational period in the social and physical domains are largely sealed off by subsequent developmental stages and therefore are not really subject to modification.

Part II

DIAGNOSIS

Chapter 5

DIAGNOSIS OF INTUITIVE AND OPERATIONAL CHARACTER STRUCTURE

Diagnosis of character structure as a practical matter is not quite as simple as we initially thought.

In Chapter 4 we discussed the three fundamental parameters of character structure. If one can identify these— the major life investment, the style of social cognition, and the overall quality of early experience of parenting—then with a reasonable congruence of the three factors one has a character structure diagnosis. This is largely how the principle author arrives at a diagnosis in both patients and nonpatients. The second author tends not to use this approach. Since either approach works, this divergence of diagnostic methods went undiscovered until we attempted to teach a nonclinician how to diagnose character structure in a normal population.

Each of us employs a different frame of reference. The first author assumes that a person is symbolic and then looks for evidence to support this assumption. This proves to be a reasonable first approximation because most of our patients and apparently most normals appear to be symbolic. The second author starts with the proposition that a patient is operational until proven otherwise and that operational and intuitive qualities are almost mutually exclusive. He also looks for the pathologic traits that ally themselves with either the operational or intuitive. The second author essentially approaches the diagnostic task the same way we first discovered our character types. Initially, we assumed that most persons were operational (something we no longer believe) and noted that patients who had obsessive–compulsive features shared little with those who were delinquent or sociopathic. It was in extrapolating to the norm that we derived the operational and intuitive character structures respectively. If the second author happens to find striking evidence of attachment behavior or of a blurring of self-object boundaries or of schizophrenic or borderline symptomatology, he recognizes he is working with a symbolic. Barring this, if a patient has intuitive characteristics, if he tends to externalize or manipulate, or if he appears to be more toward the pathological end of the intuitive continuum—if he has a history of being dishonest, impulsive, or in trouble with society—then the diagnosis of operational character is excluded. Correspondingly, a patient is not an intuitive if he presents with operational characteristics; if he is responsible and uses undoing, isolation, or intellectualization; or— at the pathological end of the operational continuum—if he has obsessive symptoms, is overly concerned about punctuality or orderliness, or is scrupulous about rules and obligations. If, however, a patient has both intuitive and operational qualities, then with few exceptions (which we will go into later) that patient is neither an intuitive nor an operational, but a mixed symbolic, a subtype of symbolic (see Chapter 4 regarding subtypes).

Generally once the second author finds a few intuitive characteristics he stops looking for operational characteristics, as he assumes the person is not an operational. He then attempts to rule out the patient's being a symbolic. He looks for evidence of role reversal in relation to caregivers, of identity problems, of attachment issues, and of preconceptual (particle-to-particle) thinking. If he fails to find symbolic traits he diagnoses the patient as an intuitive. Similarly, if the second author finds a few operational characteristics, he does not concern himself with anything other than trying to find symbolic traits. If he fails to find symbolic traits, he is dealing with an operational.

When diagnosing, more attention is paid to the defect or symptom than to what the patient is able to do well. This may seem unfair, and it probably emphasizes what is least important in treatment, but it does seem to hold true in diagnosis, where one hallucination nearly outweighs any amount of nonhallucinated thinking. Thus in character diagnosis, a characteristic of the more primitive character structure carries more diagnostic weight than a characteristic of a less primitive character structure. We view the symbolic as more primitive than the intuitive and the intuitive as more primitive than the operational. By "more primitive" we do not mean that one type is worse or less adaptive than another, but merely that one type derives from an earlier period of development and is less differentiated than the other. Thus two signs of symbolic function almost invariably establish the diagnosis of symbolic, and two signs of intuitive function largely exclude a diagnosis of operational. Superstitious thinking and a complaint of emptiness or lack of direction will largely rule out intuitive and operational as character diagnosis. Devious behavior and use of a typical intuitive defense such as externalization, denial, rationalization, manipulation, or acting out, in contrast to the operational defenses of undoing, isolation, and intellectualization will rule out the diagnosis of operational.

DIAGNOSIS OF THE INTUITIVE AND OPERATIONAL

Because the intuitive character is almost the opposite
of the operational character we may contrast the two in
terms of how they present themselves for psychotherapy
and of how they behave in psychotherapy. Whereas an
operational character's presenting complaint usually reflects issues of function and control of function, such as
concerns about sexuality, productivity, initiative, or control, an intuitive character typically presents with complaints reflecting issues of narcissistic supplies. The intuitive is concerned about whether he is or is not getting
something he likes or about whether he has missed out or
is about to miss out on something. In some cases there is
no disguise in his presentation for treatment, as he states
his global expectation from therapy: "All I want is to be
happy." When he does have defensive disguises, these
may bend inner and outer reality as he pursues narcissistic
supplies or avoidance of pain. In order to have the therapist think well of him or in order to think well of himself
he may credit himself for what he does for another, never
acknowledging either to the therapist or to himself what
he gets in return. Rationalizations are his stock in trade:
wanting some new equipment that would enhance his
position at the hospital, one intuitive said, "Money is allo-
cated two years in advance. It is free right now. Then after
you get it, you can do what you want with it. Twenty-five
thousand dollars isn't much. It is a small part of the overall budget." Wanting to get a troublesome patient out of
sight because of an imminent inspection, a program direc-
tor said, "You can put the patient into seclusion, because
schizophrenics need not to have too much stimulation."
Wanting immediate gratification, an intuitive may say, "I
can only do these things when I'm young," or "I'm too old
to wait." Reference to talk or writing as "blah, blah, blah"
or "boiler plate" may alert the therapist to the likelihood

that words have little meaning to this patient, a person with intuitive characteristics.

Operational characters may experience conflict between dependency and autonomy. Some fall into the group who have "overdosed" on autonomy, allowing themselves very little dependent gratification. Others prove to have desire for, but to be fearful or feel guilty about, autonomy. In the psychotherapeutic situation, individuals who fear or feel guilty about being more autonomous may plead ineptitude in a bid for a safe dependent role. Because of this fear or guilt they may induce the therapist to guide or support them when guidance and support are not in their best interests, or they may assume that the therapist wants to control them and keep them dependent.

An operational's complaint in contrast to the intuitives's tends to center on function. One young executive, Mr. K, complained that he was unable to "take the bull by the horns," "stick his neck out," and "throw his hat in the ring"; he was having difficulty in making the decision to apply for a "big promotion," which he had reason to believe he could get. He was the eldest in his family and often took father's place because father, "the commuter," was away from home much of the time. Mr. K was very competitive but if he were to be promoted to a position more senior than that of his supervisor, it would be as if Mr. K "had done him in." An excellent swimmer, Mr. K always finished second. Mr. K knew what he wanted: he wanted to advance. His indecision resulted from anxiety and guilt about his goals, not from changing goals as might be typical for an intuitive, or from lack of goals as might occur in a symbolic.

Mr. H was a forthright man, also an operational, who did not feel particularly anxious or guilty about autonomy. He had been separated from his wife for 6 months prior to psychotherapy. Over the course of their 9-year marriage his wife had come to resent centering her life around her husband and around his needs and wishes. She wanted to separate in order to decide whether to continue the marriage. At first the patient opposed the separation and tried to convince his wife that they should work out their problems while remaining together. She insisted on the separation. As the separation continued he began to remember and resent his wife's frequent dissatisfaction with his function as a husband and father. By the time his wife decided she wanted to resume the marriage, he was enjoying his autonomy and resisted returning to her.

Mr. H sought treatment because he felt confused. He had been raised in a traditional family in which great value was placed on family stability and the fulfillment of family roles. Although he did not want to live with his wife again, he knew he would continue to feel guilty if he did not abide by his principles and preserve the family. He felt particularly guilty about not being in the home as his young son grew up, although he spent weekends with the son. He hoped that psychotherapy would help him dissipate resentment for past wrongs, and make him more aware of his feelings so that he would recognize moments when little things bothered him and be able to express his feelings at the appropriate time, rather than dismissing incidents as trivial, thus adding to his resentment.

An operational character typically describes his problems as internal rather than external. Mr. H saw his problem as his own inability to make a decision. Initially Mr. H presented his problem as his need always to feel in control of his own actions, which resulted in his feeling threatened when his wife made certain decisions for him. He wondered how he could overcome this resentment about not being consulted. Sometimes, as with Mr. H, an operational character may think of his problem as internal and wonder what is wrong with himself or what he should do differently, when the problem is primarily external, such as an infantile wife or a treacherous superior at work.

While an operational character often presents his complaint in terms of an internal conflict, a complaint about himself, the complaint of an intuitive character usually concerns some external problem, a problem that someone else is creating for him. The intuitive character may be angry because his lover is having an affair or depressed because he was fired by an unjust employer. he sees himself as a victim of some evil that has befallen him. That may often be the case, but the intuitive does not see his complicity in the calamity. More often than not he does not come to therapy under his own motivation but is sent by someone else, sometimes under threat, such as a threat of divorce or of loss of a job. When an intuitive character presents with a complaint of depression or a loss of self-esteem, inquiry usually reveals that these conditions are attributed to an external event.

Although inclined to blame circumstances or other people for his problems, the intuitive character occasionally takes the blame himself. When he does see himself as bad, he is severe in his self-condemnation, just as he is severe in his condemnation of others. Once circumstances improve, he usually feels all right again. Often, an intuitive character does not understand how he gets into problematic situations; he is unaware of his impulsiveness, his tendency to grasp at whatever looks appealing at the moment, finding later that what looked good is not as good as it looked or that once again he has gotten himself into trouble.

Using what makes him feel good as his measure for determining right or wrong, an intuitive character may find himself at odds with another person or with society. Being in some kind of trouble may be part of his presentation for psychotherapy. A history of such troubles—that is, delinquency—may solidify the diagnosis. In any case it will usually rule out the possibility that the patient is operational.

An intuitive also almost always expects the therapist

somehow to "fix" either himself or the situation he describes. Sometimes a third party—the employer, the spouse, or in more extreme cases the probation or parole officer—is part of the treatment. Sometimes intuitive characters come to therapy on their own because of frustration at not getting something they want, e.g., frustration at losing a relationship. Typically such patients discard the therapist once they resume an outside relationship.

An operational character tends to be problem-oriented in treatment. Some operational characters will consciously or unconsciously select a problem to work on and pursue understanding of the problem within treatment or even outside the therapy sessions. Others who have difficulties in starting, continuing, or finishing an activity may reflect such impediments in their thinking or vocalizing during the treatment sessions. Since an operational character often has obsessive–compulsive or phobic traits, he may vacillate between defiance and compliance, sometimes getting "bogged down" as he strains to tell his story. Although generally observant of limits, an operational character may push them at times, e.g., coming late or not paying on time. Such behavior does not indicate poor impulse control as it does in the intuitive, but rather defiance of and autonomy from the therapist.

Intuitive characters, unlike operational characters, are not particularly interested in improving their function. Rather their efforts are toward avoiding a painful subject. They may even avoid talking about a painful subject because talking about it may make the subject seem current and more real, and the affect more intense. Although they have little investment in function per se, many intuitive characters have a know-how in regard to the world. "That is how you do it. You can buy them. You provide them a chance to extend their research. Then you can get them to offer you a teaching program." Generally those intuitives who have this know-how and who are good manipulators do not need to consult therapists.

A FIRST INTERVIEW WITH AN INTUITIVE CHARACTER

Mr. W, an intuitive character, was a salesman who was approaching his 50th birthday. He felt that he had acquired little in relationships or in business and was fearful of dying, as a number of his salesman friends had died recently. Depressed, he was unable to generate the enthusiasm he needed to face some of the negative responses of the buying public or to sell his product to prospective customers. Although he continually responded to impulse, he was facile with rationalizations and externalizations such that his responses appeared reasonable under the circumstances. Trust and distrust were major issues for him. He was untrustworthy in a number of situations and often lived on the edge of the law. He also had major difficulty knowing whom to trust. Especially in his work life, he continually manipulated others, and yet repeatedly allowed himself to be manipulated.

He was not task-oriented in the interview in the sense of being directed toward increased understanding. At times he was vague, which resulted in the therapists's failure to understand him. Yet Mr. W did not correct the therapist, as understanding was not an important issue for him. Early in the first interview, Mr. W considered that he might have a defect, but during most of the hour he pointed out that it was unwise to trust and recounted examples in which he was abused by others. He spent much of the hour arguing his case and defending himself. He viewed his troubles as coming from outside.

In the beginning of the first interview, considerable time was expended in a gentle fencing dialogue between Mr. W and the therapist. Each tried to get the other to choose a topic. Mr. W said "there is so much to choose from." Mr. W continues after the fencing:

Patient: Well, I guess I'm a restless sort of fellow and I haven't had any satisfaction out of things that I should have. And come to this period of my life and I've got a big zero. It sort of annoys me.

This is an apt description of himself as impulsive and having attained for himself little that lasts. We start to think that he is intuitive or intuitive symbolic.

Patient: I don't seem to have, to be able to make, a close relationship with anybody, you know.

One of his chief complaints.

Therapist: Not with anybody?
Patient: No, I don't even have a close relationship with Him.
Therapist: At all?
Patient: No, nobody at all.
Therapist: Uh huh.
Patient: Maybe I'm too suspicious of people. I don't know. I don't know what is wrong, but I know I wouldn't be here.

Trust is an issue. It is unlikely that he is operational. This appears to be an example of immanent justice or end-stage reasoning, i.e., intuitive style social cognition. He implies that it is only because he is seeing a psychiatrist that there is something wrong with him. Clearly he is intuitive or intuitive symbolic.

Patient: But I just don't have the closeness with people that I should have, not even with my own children, not even with my wives. So there must be something missing here and if it happens consistently, maybe there is something wrong with me. I don't know.

He has mentioned his main problems and is considering that he may have a defect. However, for the remainder of the hour he externalizes, a typical intuitive defense.

Therapist: When you say you don't have the close relationships with them that you'd like, are you referring to anything specific?
Patient: No, in general. I've been disappointed so much in close

relationships that maybe I have the wrong idea of people and hold these ideals too long.

He externalizes. There is no longer something wrong with him. He is merely too idealistic. He then cites an example in which he did trust a business associate to whom he felt close, who betrayed him. Thus he rationalizes his distrust. Rationalization is another typical intuitive defense.

Patient: Like when I first got into sales, a fellow by the name of Bud, that I had a lot of confidence in and he taught me my sales, and he did a lot for me. And I guess, you know, when we first go out he did things that I didn't expect him to do for me. And maybe it kind of took me aback and I liked him for it, you know, and always appreciated it. And two years later I went into business with him on a very, very small scale, and the guy turned out to be a bad apple. He didn't shoulder his part of the responsibility for the work or financial responsibility, or anything. He let me bear the brunt of the whole thing. And then when I suggested we break it up, I said, "Now you owe me money on the whole deal." And we were dickering on how much he owed me. And it was only a matter of a few hundred dollars, you know. So rather than dicker with him, because it hurt me to dicker with him, so I, as a very ridiculous thing to say, said, "Don't you think you at least owe me a hundred?" He said, "Oh, yeah." I was mad at the man's way of saying, "Well let's make it a hundred," you know. And he did make me a promissory note for a hundred and never paid me off. And it strained my relationship with him. I haven't seen him for years, you known, since the first time. And I had this close relationship with him on a different plane than I had before. And he turned out to be a gossipy old guy, you know. It really destroyed my image of the guy, you know. He was a disappointment to me. That's why I'm afraid to get close to people, because they always turn out to be a disappointment.

He has not explained to the therapist that he is about to start another business with Bud. This is not revealed until the next interview. This probably evidences his distrust of the therapist.

Therapist: How do you account for that you didn't spot that about him earlier?

Patient: He did nothing to indicate it to me. He'd always been helpful, and everything's good. But I didn't know him that closely. His relationship then was, I'm a salesman and he's a sales manager. I guess I expect him to be human naturally. I know some of his human shortcomings, that he had a wife and kids, and I believe he didn't take care of them.

He knew his associate's dishonesty in other situations. Somehow he was unable to use this information in his abiding appraisal of him, hence in any new momentary appraisal. This discontinuity in valuation of an object is typical of intuitive social cognition.

Therapist: And that didn't alert you that maybe he would be irresponsible in a relationship with you too?

Patient: Well, I figured that maybe that's his problem. Maybe his wife didn't treat him right, or something. Maybe that's why he's not assisting with his wife as he should.

He rationalizes his misjudgment.

Patient: That's why he had all the spare time. That's why he's in this type of work and maybe his work is taking his time. . . . I didn't feel at that time, but I never thought of it until everything else came to a head. It seems like a person's gotta be Gestapo-like, you know, in order to make relationships with people. I didn't think it would actually be that complicated.

Therapist: What do you mean, Gestapo?

Patient: Well, it's a. . . . Well, before I can become friends with you, for instance, I want to interrogate you very closely, check you very carefully, and I can't take you at what our relationship is at the moment. See? I base my relationship with a person on what we do now. And if everything we do now is all right and somebody says something's bad about you, I'll defend you on this basis. Actually I can't speak from outside of what our relationship is. Although it is limited, I can indicate what kind of man he is.

He is saying it is proper to judge by the view presented. One should not prejudge someone. He rationalizes the fact that he does not coordinate what he knows from the past or from another person's point of view. He takes surface for essence.

Therapist: But you mean there was nothing in your relationship with that man up to a certain point that would have indicated what he was like?

Patient: It may be and I didn't recognize it. We never discussed his wife and his children. I never asked about it.

Therapist: Uh, huh. I mean in your relationship together there wasn't anything you could have spotted?

Patient: No. He was very helpful. He was very helpful. He had an axe to grind. Naturally, the more I make, the more he makes.

He was aware of his sales manager's motives, but does not use this knowledge to moderate his surface view of his sales manager.

Patient: He was very conscientious about it. He was very good at it. And he had a very nice, pleasing personality. I liked him very much.

He judges on the basis of appearance. He then gives another example of his (momentarily) placing his trust in someone and being disappointed.

Patient: I just happen to run into all these people that are real tough. A screwy incident comes to mind right now. I ran around with this girl, and she was pretty well off. And I was more or less struggling. In my work I need a calculator. And she can buy it wholesale. I said, "Good, would you mind if I do this, you know, through your account." I say, "I'll be frank with you. I couldn't pay you all cash now, but I can pay you later. And I would appreciate it, if you can get it for me now, because I need it now." She said, "Swell." She said, "That's all right. Take your time and pay me later." And I said, "Oh, I really appreciate this." So I think it was my birthday coming up, or something. So she was feeling pretty mellow one evening. And she said, "You know something," she says, "I know you're struggling to get ahead and everything like that and I think I'll just let you have that calculator. It's not too expensive. I'll let you have it for your birthday." Well, you know you are taken aback by something like that, somebody gives you just something like that.

He was truly moved by the offer, as he was by Bud's helping him.

Patient: I said, "Well, gee, you shouldn't." And she said, "Well, then, I won't. I've decided it might be too expensive for you. I'll get you something else." I said, "Well, that's fine." So I said, "You shouldn't spend so much money," or something like that. She said, "That's very considerate." She said, "I won't." Well here it is. I've already accepted in my mind. You see what I mean? And she turns right around and says, "I am not going to give it to you." I never expected it, to begin with. She blew my mind with this. I don't like people like her. You give me something and then take it back. Then you're no good. Don't ever give it to me and then take it back.

He judges by current action, not crediting the intent of another.

Therapist: Are you talking about, it's kind of like when you're depending on somebody and then they kind of pull the rug out from under you?

Patient: Yeah, that's dirty. Don't never offer it to me. I never asked for it. I ask for so much help, this much. Right? Give me more and then take it back again is like manipulating me, right?

Actually, he was manipulating her. This is a projection—a typical defense of an intuitive or a symbolic.

Therapist: Do you think she was doing that? Or that she . . .

Patient: I don't understand what her motive was. Well, I think it was in a moment of weakness, she overextended herself. After she uttered it, she regretted it. But people like that show their character, I think.

He understands her intent, but his understanding does not modify his disappointment. All he knows is he did not get what he wanted. He is describing the kind of difficulty he has when he associates with someone who is not like himself, someone who may vacillate. Later the therapist learns this was an important relationship in his life. This would not be apparent to the therapist on the basis of Mr. W's casual style in introducing the subject, just as it is not apparent to the therapist that Mr. W's involvement with Bud is a current issue. Often only in retrospect is one able to recognize the intuitive's true concerns. It is clear, however, that all concerns are in terms of what he is currently getting and not getting.

Patient: You know, everybody thought I should have married her and so did she. But because of this incident it changed my mind. Instead of progressing, I went backwards from my relationship with her, which I feel kind of guilty about, because she didn't have to give it to me. She could have taken it back, but I am annoyed by it. I don't trust her because then she will give me other things that she will take back also. I don't like an "Indian giver." Whatever you offer to give me, give it to me. Don't take it back. I can't have a relationship with a person like that. And these people criticize me all the time but she was a hard person to get along with. People say I should have married her. Why should I?

The patient is letting the therapist know how he functions, how to treat him. Do not make promises if you cannot keep them.

Later in this interview Mr. W recounted some memories of his mother's neglecting him and his brother when they were young. In an unstructured first interview of an intuitive character we do not expect the patient to describe in detail such parental neglect. However, Mr. W's history of neglect helped confirm his diagnosis.

A FIRST INTERVIEW WITH AN OPERATIONAL CHARACTER

Ms. L, an operational character, was a forthright, intelligent, plain-looking young woman who had recently begun graduate school. In the past month, she had begun having involuntary, murderous thoughts that frightened her. These thoughts were not accompanied by any conscious anger. Ms. L, generally detached from her feelings, found it difficult to describe her feelings or to label them accurately. She confused anxiety with depression. She was thinking- rather than feeling- or action-oriented. She made fine distinctions in her narrative and was relieved by insight or intellectualization. She used undoing almost constantly.

The unconscious resentment that culminated in her murderous thoughts was stimulated by feelings of being controlled by her teachers, her boyfriend, and her mother. In this interview she indicates that she attributed control over her own actions to her boyfriend, that he generally was uninclined to force his will on her, but she felt as if he did. She was much concerned about being in control of her function, and resented the possibility of someone else controlling her.

The therapist was somewhat overactive in Ms. L's first interview.

Patient: Well, I've been really depressed but it's a different kind of depression than I've ever had. And that's why I started to get really worried, cause usually when I get depressed, it's the fact that something happened. And I can say, well, I'm depressed but this happened, you know. And I see sort of a cause and effect relationship.

Insight or intellectualization helps her. Both fit an operational. She would not be as troubled if she could explain the reason for her depression.

Patient: But I just feel really bad, and I've been, I don't know, it's really hard to talk. I mean it's real hard to say what it is that I feel, but I've been feeling . . . I really have morbid, although not violent, thoughts. They're not violent. I don't see myself doing it, but I think to myself that I have capability of doing, you know, things that I consider really hideous.

Therapist: What are some of these things?

Patient: Well, like knives really bother me. If I'm around knives, I really get nervous. I don't get nervous but I think, well, I can pick one up and stab somebody with it. But I don't actually see myself doing it, but it's just, you know, it's really scary. I mean I'm really upset about it.

Undoing. The second author would be thinking obsessive–compulsive, hence operational, because of the defenses she uses. Hereafter he would be looking for symbolic characteristics and would be surprised if he found intuitive ones, because the two types of characteristics generally are mutually exclusive.

Therapist: Do you see a knife and think, "I could really stab somebody with it?"

Patient: Yes, well, and I've been living with my boyfriend and most of it is directed . . . against him. But I think not because of him, but because he is the only person I'm really around.

Undoing.

Therapist: So does that mean then that your thoughts when you see a knife are, "I could pick this up and kill him with it, or how . . ."

Patient: I don't really. Yes. See that's the hard thing. I don't really say I could pick it up and do it. I just say it could be done. I mean it's really hard to say what the difference is, but naturally I'll be scared.

She makes a fine distinction as she undoes constantly.

Patient: I mean I'm really, you known, cause I think that's, that's incredible, that I could possibly even have that kind of thought. It's something I've never had to deal with before, and I don't know what's brought it on all of a sudden, but I just started graduate school, and it seems to have started before then but not significantly before then, which is like a month. I would say it's been about a month anyhow. Now it really didn't bother me a lot until this weekend. I just, you know, I couldn't, it seemed like I had just broken down. You know my defenses couldn't handle . . . I couldn't say to myself any more, "Stop thinking that. That's a silly thought," which was basically what I was trying to do, and I just, I couldn't do it anymore. I just, you know, felt really broken.

She uses intellectualization to suppress or repress when she brands it a silly thought.

Therapist: You mean it got worse this weekend or . . .

Patient: Yes, it got worse. Well, that's I'm not sure if it got worse or I just stopped coping with it. It don't think it was any worse, but I sort of let it get control, you know. I just didn't put up any resistance, and I'm really getting real upset about it now.

Again in her undoing she makes fine distinctions and takes some responsibility for her problems.

Therapist: Uh, huh. But just knives, or is there something else that gives you this feeling?

Patient: Uh, scissors. In fact, it's not all knives. That's another thing. That I was thinking about today, is that it's not, it doesn't seem to be all of them. It's just certain ones. I mean, I don't know. I don't understand it, you know, and I have general, like I mean it's, you know, I'll go someplace, and I'll say, I don't know if I should. My mother is really morbid. My mother is the kind of person who (she lives in New Bedford, so I don't see her often), but she is the kind of person who reads all the murders in the newspapers.

An object for identification? Identification as part of symptom formation may occur in any character type. She has been trying to figure out her problem. She is task- or function-oriented. She is probably an operational but could be an operational symbolic.

Patient: And I've known this, that, you know, I don't like that, but yet, and it seems to be that when I visit her I am conscious of it. Like this, I don't know if there is any correlation, but like this weekend before last I had been, I had visited her. Then this weekend is when I felt really bad. And I sort of feel it taking over. As long as I am busy and as long as I'm talking, and concentrating on something, I'm OK, I don't feel it, but when my mind starts to sort of wander, you know, I think I've talked myself into it, too. I have that feeling.

Focused thinking as a coping mechanism. Thinking is typical of an operational's coping techniques, whereas action is typical of those of an intuitive.

Therapist: How do you mean?

Patient: Well, I mean I have the feeling that I could, that I could have stopped it at one point, and that I almost did, but maybe I enjoy it? Maybe there's something about that you, maybe I like it, I liked it, you know? Who knows why? But maybe now I am, uh, sort of enjoying it, not consciously. I mean it's making me miserable, but I mean maybe, maybe at another level I am sort of enjoying it. Maybe it's making me feel really real, you know, rather than sort of counteracting that. I don't know.

She has an observing ego. She takes some responsibility for the symptom, and she tolerates her bad characteristics. All this suggests she is operational, not intuitive and not a sick symbolic who might be confused rather than having any of the above characteristics. Her reference to feeling "real" is a possible identity concern, although it is more a matter of being alienated from her feelings. It could raise the question of whether we are dealing with an operational symbolic and not a pure operational.

Therapist: You don't seem very upset.

Patient: I'm not when I talk about it. That's the strangest thing, I am not, like I've been talking, like I told my fiancee. So, it's easier if I just call him that [fiancee].

She feels guilty about living with her boyfriend. She calls it by another name and then undoes it, calling it what it is.

Patient: But I told him about it, cause this weekend I was really upset. I woke up in the middle of the night, and my mind just clicked like that, and started thinking it, and I was really upset and really scared. I almost was at a point where I could, not that I felt that I could do it. But I kept thinking about it, you know. And I feel that if I keep thinking about it, then maybe I could do it eventually. But anyway I was really upset so I told him about it. And I was in tears and even when I called here yesterday. I was really upset just thinking about it, but yet I can talk about it rationally and say, "How ridiculous!" That's why I think I have, that I could have control, but I'm sort of, for some reason, not controlling.

Issues of control of her function. Control is a major issue for an

operational, but may also be important for an operational
symbolic.

Therapist: Control over the thoughts?

Patient: Over the thoughts, right, cause it's basically thought. I
mean that's all it is, is thoughts. I feel that maybe I could,
but I can't any more, you know. I'm just, I feel like I've lost
control.

Therapist: You mean overwhelmed by them?

Patient: Yeah. I am. That's what I feel. I mean if I sit at home, I'll
come home from school and sit down and do my home-
work. And my mind is not concentrating completely on
what I'm doing. It's you know, it will, I can feel my, I mean
it's really, I don't know, you know, it's just got me. And
really, I'm in a bad position, you know.

Therapist: So it seems that it's not just knives and scissors. It also
starts at other times, like in the middle of the night or while
you are studying?

Patient: Yeah, right. I would say that they are a little bit different. I mean it's not like I, I don't know, it's really hard to
describe it. It's really hard to say what it, you know, what it
actually is that I'm thinking when I think. Well, one thing, I
can give you one specific example because I remember this
one because it was . . . I had felt good all day and we went
out and we went for a walk. I don't know if you know
where Halstead Street is, but there's really pretty houses
there, and we walk there occasionally, and it's really nice,
you know. It's a nice warm evening Saturday night, and we
go there, and I for no reason (I mean I was feeling good
otherwise) I got the thought, "This would be a good place
to dump a body." I mean, you known, what a ridiculous
thing. But I've always, I was hesitant in talking about it
because, you know, if I can do it myself, if I can help myself, it's better than, you know.

She prefers to be autonomous, to be in control of her own
function.

Patient: That's, that's, you know, it's much more desirable than
having to go elsewhere, and since I've never gone anyplace.

She uses "go elsewhere" or "anyplace else" peculiarly. She

means go to someone else such as a therapist. This idiosyncratic use of words might cause us to think she is symbolic.

Patient: That isn't my first thought. And I've always liked murder mysteries. I've always, you know, and I've always liked things like that. And now they scare the shit out of me. Now I get terrified when I see one, or if I am watching a movie and it's a murder movie, I get really scared. I just, you know. . .

In liking murder mysteries she is similar to her mother, a possible gender identity and oedipal issue. In any symptomatology there is undifferentiation, limited loss of ego boundaries. In this instance, the patient is taken over by the movie.

Therapist: You were feeling very good that day, but you were depressed the day before, uh?

Patient: Yeah, and I had the depressed feeling during the day on Saturday. But during the evening, well we went out. And I had some wine. And that made me feel really good. That made me forget completely. And I felt fine at that point, you know. And then just suddenly, just like, you know, I don't know. Well, I am depressed now in a way. I think I don't feel right, like my heart is beating fast, right now. And I feel nervous.

She is not a good diagnostician of her feelings. She is anxious, not "depressed," since she describes being nervous and having a rapid heartbeat. Isolation of affect is a typical obsessive, hence operational, defense.

Patient: And I don't feel the same way that I would normally do. I mean I feel a bit different right now. Oh, I think I mean by depression in this particular circumstance is that I feel really funny. And I'm really sort of unhappy with myself for being this way, you know. It's sort of self-fulfilling in a way. You . . . I cry. And that hasn't helped, you know, that I've been so upset, and has made me feel, you know, bad. But it's almost physical. My stomach has been churning, like I would feel if I were extremely nervous. And it's you know, I can just, I mean I'll just sit and I'll let my mind wander and it will wander to morbid things, you know, and it's just. . . .

Therapist: And that really scares you?

Patient: Yeah, it does really. It really does scare me now cause I think that it's really, uh, I mean I can't understand it, and I can't, I can't deal with it anymore.

She can't understand. She can't control.

Patient: I just, I am really scared. And I think that's the best way. That's why I decided that one night when I woke up in the middle of the night I was, I was really scared. It was terrifying. And I don't know, you know, I don't know what to do any more.

Therapist: What kind of things bring on this depression that you talk about?

It is unclear why the therapist went back to "depression" after clarifying the feeling as fear or anxiety by saying "scares you."

Patient: Well, I don't know. It seems like it basically just comes on itself. It's almost like, well like when I woke up this morning, I felt depressed. I just, I felt funny, you know. I didn't, I can't say I mean, I haven't thought of it as being suicidal, but I can see where if it kept on for the next year, I wouldn't know what else to do.

Her suicidal impulse is a long way off.

Patient: I wouldn't know how else to solve it. I mean I can't, I can't continually, you know, it's just overwhelming. And I don't know why it started.

Understanding would make a difference.

Patient: I don't know what really, I mean it just seems to be my defenses are down. And it just sort of floods in and I can't stop it, or I don't want to.

She tries to take responsibility for her symptoms.

Patient: Or whatever or for whatever reason, it just does it. And I mean I have never had that when I woke up in the morning. I can almost feel it turn on in a way.

Therapist: The depression?

Patient: Yeah, the depression, right. I just sort of, I can almost feel it coming over me, yeah. I don't know.

Therapist: But what comes to your mind when you feel that coming over you the first thing in the morning?

Patient: I just feel just terrible. I just feel really bad. A lot of it I'm sure is guilt. I mean I haven't ever really experienced what I would consider conscious guilt. But I'm sure a lot of it is that I can think these things about Bob, you know, that I could even want to hurt him. And I'm sure I feel very guilty about it. Maybe it's that, you know. Maybe it's guilt, but I don't know what to call it other than depression. But it's general malaise. It means I just feel funny.

"Guilt" appears to be the right word. Having such thoughts violates her code. She appears to have an autonomous social-ego.

Therapist: What's happening between you and your boyfriend right now?
Patient: Well, I try to think of everything, uh, I've tried to think of everything.
Therapist: I know you've thought a lot about this. I can tell.
Patient: Yeah. Well, nothing that I know of. He's, we're both in school. I just started graduate school, and he's finishing his M.D. this year. So I think a lot of it is due to the fact that . . . well, as a student you probably know what it's like. I mean you live on $500 a month, and you don't, I don't have time to go out. I don't. We don't have a television, I mean I think it's in a way maybe I'm just tired of the whole thing. And, you know, I'm using this as a way of sort of breaking it.
Therapist: You're tired of the whole thing?
Patient: Of sort of coping, you know, having to live on, not being able to go out. (I love to go out to dinner.) Not being able to go out to dinner because we can't afford it; living in a crummy apartment because that's all we can afford; uh, not being able to go out just general because of time, you know, because we have to study. I mean, I don't know, I think maybe a lot of it is that he has a lot of control over . . . I mean he's the one who says we have to study tonight.

She resents being controlled.

Patient: And maybe in a way I resent that. I'm the kind of person . . . I'm not that dedicated to study. I mean I'll go out if I want to go out and have a good time. But he's really much more dedicated than I am, and sort of forces me to study.

Maybe that's part of it. And also he doesn't like to go out. He will go out. He does go out. I think the thing is he says he doesn't like to go out but does it. And I say I like to go out and also do it. You know he's not used to it. When he was growing up he never went out with his, with his family. They didn't live that way. And part of the thing was they also didn't have the money. But it may be that, you know, that that's why I'm taking it out on him, that I feel he is keeping me oppressed. I don't know.

She undoes her feeling of oppression with "I don't know." Unfortunately the therapist has trouble restraining himself again.

Therapist: How do you deal with it?
Patient: With not being able to go out?
Therapist: No, well, with feeling oppressed.
Patient: Well, I never really felt oppressed. I mean that's the thing. If you ask me how we're getting along, we get along fine. I mean I haven't noticed any change in our relationship, and I don't feel oppressed consciously.

She must deduce her feelings, isolation of affect.

Patient: I mean I do about little things, you know, like I have to cook dinner. But we have sort of worked it out that he washes the dishes. But I mean it's still in a way, even though we worked it out in terms of actual work done, he, I still feel it's my responsibility, even though he does the work. I'm sort of like the supervisor, if you want to call it that. You know, I tell him, I don't have to tell him to wash the dishes, but I still feel that the house is my responsibility basically even though he will clean and everything like that. But I don't really feel oppressed. I mean I don't feel that he's holding me back from anything that I want to do. I mean he wouldn't do that you know. He's not that way. But he and I feel that it's much more subtle than that. I feel held back even though I am not held back. And I don't know why. It's not that I would be doing anything different if he weren't there. But just his presence in a way makes me feel held back. And it's not just him. It's also going to school.

She attributes control of her function to her boyfriend, a failure of differentiation at the level of function. So far we have not seen evidence of self-object undifferentiation (except on p. 87) or attachment concerns. Any preconceptual cognition has been unconvincing. She recognizes her problem as internal although her boyfriend's presence activates it.

Patient: I would be held back by school also 'cause that's really time consuming. So I don't feel . . . the thing that's really bothering me is I don't feel any cause for what's going on. And it's like it sort of coincides with going to visit my mother, but nothing, you know, specific about it.

She feels oppressed by her mother, boyfriend, and school. But all the causal and affective connections are missing, presumably due to isolation and compartmentalization.

Therapist: What about school, huh, what's happening in school?

The patient discusses graduate school, where she feels constantly challenged.

Patient: . . . It's very, I think the main thing about it is that in undergraduate school the pressure is not constant. The pressure sort of came and went, like in the beginning you had to do a paper. There was pressure. And at the end when you had finals or had a term paper, there was pressure. But now it is every single day, there's pressure.

An obsessive struggle.

Patient: You have to read the homework every single day, I mean you can't goof off. If you do make a fool of yourself, I mean you really blow it and you feel extremely, you know there's a lot of pressure to do well and that if you don't do well, you're going to flunk out. And so you have the feeling that if you don't do it, you don't do your homework one day, that you know, you're gonna flunk out not that directly. But there's been cautions about "Don't get behind in the reading. You'll be sorry if you do." It is a lot of pressure, but I haven't really been feeling it. In fact I think part of it is that I expected it to be a lot worse than it has turned out to be . . .

She undoes her whole previous statement regarding the pressure of school.

She describes the Socratic method used at her school, and her procrastination in regard to homework.

Patient: . . . I manufacture chores around the house. "Oh, the floor needs mopping," you know, the usual goof off and that's my usual weekend, which I . . . In fact, I haven't really felt much pressure about school. That's why I can't really relate it directly to my falling apart. You know, I don't know, and the thing is I can talk about it very rationally when I'm not feeling it. And as long as I am talking and as long as my mind is sort of occupied, I don't feel it. I feel normal. I feel good now, you know.

Talking and thinking helps.

Therapist: But when you are studying you don't feel your mind is occupied?

Patient: Ah . . . it is while I am studying. But there is that preliminary period where I sit down. And it will take me maybe 20 minutes to get myself into gear. You know I have to straighten the paper and the pencils.

Her compulsive ritual does not suffice to contain her resentment at being forced to function.

Patient: In that 20 minutes I am not occupied and not concentrating. I think that this is another thing that bothers me. Why I am very ambivalent about my, not my dedication, but sort of I'm really afraid of, I'm not really afraid, but I am sure afraid of failing. And there's always and to me while I am . . . It's like nothing I've ever done and I'm sort of afraid I'll get through and not like it and still be miserable in the field you know, find that it is something that I just don't like [short pause], right now I think I am turning my thinking into a very negative thing. I may not be doing anything different than I was before, but it's just turned negatively. I mean not turning into positive thoughts, like how I can save the human race. I'm not thinking like that now.

It sounds as if saving the human race was a reaction formation that has broken down and whose breakdown stimulated punitive behavior.

Patient: And I think another thing, too. This problem is that I tend to punish people in little ways. I mean that is something Bob has picked up on. You know, I tend to punish him.

The example that the patient proceeds to give of punishing someone is "punishment" of her mother. At age 23 Ms. L claims she did this by moving out from mother's home. Ms. L's mother partially supports Ms. L financially. A current complaint Ms. L has about mother is that she is subject to her mother's taste (which is the "same" as her own) when they shop together and mother buys her clothing. She then asserts that she cannot rely on her father, who at one point left the family, but who long since reinitiated contact with her and remains eager to see her whenever her schedule permits. It is consistent with her operational character structure that her parents are interested in her and care for her, although they may be controlling.

We saw no hint of intuitive characteristics during this interview with Ms. L. At the end of the interview we believed there was still a possibility that the patient might be symbolic, but that was not the case in subsequent interviews.

Chapter 6

DIAGNOSIS OF SYMBOLIC
CHARACTER STRUCTURE

Our usual patient is a symbolic character who comes for
treatment commonly because his connection to some person or role has been broken or is threatened. Such occur-
rences as retirement, death of a spouse, breakup of a relationship, or departure of the last child from home may
precipitate in the symbolic not only a feeling of loss but
also a loss of self-definition. Some symbolic characters
complain of feeling fragmented, whereas others complain
of feeling empty, adrift, abandoned, or of having no direction. Some seem to experience emotion as if it were an
excruciatingly painful physical experience. For example,
one patient still felt the death of her father two years previously as "an open sore that would not heal over."

Sometimes a symbolic character describes having centered around or having been as one with another person,
in a kind of dual unity reminiscent of the early symbiotic
relationship with the mother (Mahler, 1968). Not infrequently the other person with whom a symbolic is so close
is also a symbolic. One patient referred to her relationship
with her husband as their being in a "pink cloud" together. (Thus there are some clear advantages to being

symbolic, just as there are other advantages to being one of the other character types.)

Symbolic characters often use words that reflect their investment in attachment. "Hooked up," "connected," and "feeling cut off" are terms typically used by a symbolic. Symbolic characters may say, as may intuitives, that they need "feedback," that the therapists they had spoken to who had not talked to them had been unhelpful and "were not even in the room" and that "one might as well talk to the wall." Such therapists do not allow a connection. This type of patient may indicate that mostly what he wants is for the therapist to "be there" with him.

Not every symbolic character seeks treatment because of problems integral to his character structure. Nonetheless when he comes to work on a non-character-related symptom or issue, he usually reveals a precipitant that involves attachment. Sometimes, having made a new attachment, he plans to break off from someone he has been connected to in the past. He must deal with his concern that the other person will be hurt. He may need permission to discard his former lover. In all cases, attachment to the therapist—sometimes sought, sometimes guarded against—will be part of the treatment situation even when it is not the principle focus of treatment.

The case material in this chapter is suggestive of the variation in the presentation of symbolic characters. A symbolic character near the normal end of the continuum, who functions well in society but seeks psychotherapy in order to work on a particular issue, may not show evidence of obvious preconceptual social cognition. Sometimes the cognition may be inferred from the issues presented.

Two young women, an attorney and a program administrator, presented similar issues. Each of them had two men interested in marriage and each had been unable to decide which man to choose. The attorney was eager to marry and start a family. One of her suitors shared all of her values, was warm and caring, but had little initiative. She had persuaded him to go to professional school and had chosen his area of specialization but he was now indecisive about where to practice. The other man, an Ivy League graduate at the top of his profession who was widely published and intellectually stimulating, often was outraged at her style of dress, called her a "hippie," and scolded her because she did not confine her work to work hours. He was "mean of spirit" and "ungenerous." Sexual intercourse was not satisfying with the first man, with whom she had lived for a number of years, but was good with the second. She looked at these men as though they were a collection of attributes or parts, each part having a certain weight which she attempted to put on a scale. The first man represented safety, suburbia, the house, the small town she came from, and the provincial school she had attended. The second man represented venturing out into the scary but exciting world—the challenge of the possible. He was what she herself always had hoped to become—the "top of the heap." She felt that the man she chose would determine the part of herself she would develop. This feeling implied that she herself was not a coherent whole and that whatever person or situation she attached herself to would set her course and define her. The first man had the same ethnic background as she, which she felt might give their children a certain "blandness," whereas the second man was of a racial minority, which she felt would give their children "definition." This is perhaps an example of preconceptual thinking as she confused the concrete with the abstract. Although we were reasonably certain that she was symbolic because of the above clues and the quality of the shifts in her view of the two men and what they represented to her, giving her direction hence definition,[15] there was little clear-cut evidence of preconceptual social cognition before she chose her man and left treatment.

The program administrator was in a similar situation.

One man represented warmth, but was not particularly intellectually stimulating. The other, with whom she had lived previously for 4 years, represented excitement and intellectual stimulation but was domineering and often "squelched" her. This man, the "squelcher," accused her of seeing him only in terms of his parts. Whichever man she chose, she was afraid she would make a mistake. If she chose the "squelcher," she would be discontent because he would always be diminishing her, but if she chose the warm one, she felt she would be "missing out" on something. With the "squelcher," she would feel excited, but insecure. With the warm man she would feel secure, but unfulfilled. She wished she could marry him, have children, and then, after the children were grown, go back to the "squelcher." She would have liked to have "the good parts of each."

Although the therapist was aware of this young woman's issues of attachment and her inability to function unattached, there was for months no clear evidence of preconceptual social cognition, except for her attitude toward these men. Six months into treatment she told the therapist she had become so frustrated by not knowing which man to chose that she had consulted the tarot cards. She revealed that she always used tarot cards and other magical problem-solving methods (consulting I Ching or a fortune teller) when she felt "stuck" or confused about a decision. She told the therapist in detail the messages the cards had given her and all the other signs that predicted she would choose the "squelcher." She subsequently told this man that she wanted to make a commitment to marriage. Although still ambivalent, she acted upon this decision because she trusted the tarot cards.

Preconceptual reasoning is difficult, as it was in these patients, to recognize. At times it may be inferred from a patient's behavior. Instead of trying to figure out what they want to do by mentally weighing the pros and cons as did the two women just mentioned, others may move from place to place, or may start and quit jobs or schools.[16] Sometimes their preconceptual processing may be inferred from the confusion they cause in the therapist as they jump from one part of their story to another, with no apparent order. They may inject random observations of something happening on the street or of something that happened on the way to the session. Sometimes they free-associate to words that they or the therapist use or even to noises from outside the office.

Sometimes only a patient's "off the cuff" remarks reveal his preconceptual thinking. He may not hear these remarks himself. Prior to telling some incident he may remark: "Things always happen in threes" or "What can you expect of a Pisces?" or "It's funny, I was thinking about her when the phone rang and it was she." One such remark has little meaning, but after a number of such asides, it is reasonable for the therapist to conclude that he is dealing with a symbolic character. People who frequently use "because" may be connecting things that have no cause–effect relationship. When a therapist's ear is attuned to listening for such constructions it is easier to hear them.

Symbolics tend to use intuitive (narcissistic) defenses: denial, projection, externalization, and rationalization. They may however use operational (obsessive–compulsive) defenses instead or as well. When a patient uses both narcissistic and obsessive defenses it is likely he is a symbolic, just as when a patient has both intuitive and operational characteristics it is likely he is a symbolic. The symbolic patient's defenses, often not facile, may be obvious or ineffectual. With defenses being ineffectual, ego boundaries are vulnerable and affect is intense. Sometimes a symbolic will confuse abstract with concrete, e.g., understand the symbol as the thing. Trust–distrust is a significant issue for both the intuitive and the symbolic.

It should be noted that, except for complaints reflecting attachment and preconceptual cognition (including problems with identity), the presenting complaints of symbolic characters are generally no different from the complaints of the other two character types. Although there is a natural alliance of obsessive disorder with the operational and of the behavior disorder with the intuitive, even if a patient presents as either of these, one should be alert to the likelihood that the patient will prove to be symbolic, simply because of the greater frequency of symbolic patients.

A FIRST INTERVIEW WITH A SYMBOLIC CHARACTER

Ms. J is less well-functioning than the previous examples in this chapter, and is accordingly easier to diagnose. She was a 23-year-old college student, who understood that her parents saw her as a cute, smart, little blond girl who would fulfill their expectations and bring credit to them. She tended to form symbiotic attachments, and she experienced raw, passive depressed states or grandiose, somewhat paranoid, withdrawn states.

She talked about feeling that she was not a whole person. She described herself as a person who circles and centers around another person and as one with no identity of her own. She went to college because she thought that this is what everybody did and because her parents were happy that she was to become a teacher. She said she felt unable to handle what was happening to her and felt "panic" when she moved to a new place and did not know whom she would be "hooked up to." She spoke of feelings of superiority, particularly at the time when she could not talk to anyone else and felt a lack of distinction between herself and the universe. These feelings coincided with her being nonfunctional. Her conflict about whether or not to attach herself to another person gave her the most trouble.

Therapist: Where would you like to begin?

Patient: Well, I guess I should tell you first why I'm here. One important thing that I want to say is that I'm just going to be in town for 2½ months. I feel that I could wait, but I feel that it would better if I started with the things that were bothering me now.

An overall air of trying to convince somebody of something is conveyed by her voice.

Patient: Right now I am in a situation where I feel that I have been doing fine. I'm really having no trouble at all and I have been moving along fine.

Denial.

Patient: But some things that have happened to me in the past are starting to bother me again, but I really feel that now is the time that I'll be able to handle it better.

Rationalization. Her use of denial and rationalization makes us think she is intuitive or intuitive symbolic, not operational.

Patient: Let's see. Well, this is what I really think is starting to bother me. Two years ago I was out here. I'd been going to school in Oregon for 2 years. I went on a work–study program. I came out here with my boyfriend and I was planning on leaving the country and I was prepared to go to Holland to a specialty school. When I came out here, that was the last time I was going to see him or anything.

It later becomes clear that issues of merger and attachment were involved. She will now speak of a great deal of moving around, and recount four examples of how she felt at the mercy of the surround, (i.e., of her pregnancy, his mother, her father, and her friend). Because of her vulnerability to the surround, we will start to think she is symbolic, probably intuitive symbolic.

Patient: Then in June I went home to work for a couple of months, and he went to Arizona. When I got home I found out that I was pregnant. I didn't know what to do, and he didn't know what to do. We didn't want to get married or anything. He was going to come to Detroit, where I was at the time, and we were going to work something out and we didn't really have any idea. The night he was supposed to come, he called up and said that his father had died the night before. I don't think at the time I was really caught up in him, because I really was so afraid for myself and what was going to happen to me. Then I went out there, and we talked to his mother. She really didn't have any sort of solutions for us. I think I wanted to get married. He didn't. His mother definitely wanted him to go to college, finish college, which would have been pretty hard, if we had got married. We decided to go back and talk to my parents who absolutely . . . Well my father absolutely insisted that we get married.

Was getting married the solution Ms. J wanted? Or was it the solution that suited her father and met his emotional needs? The latter possibility would fit with a symbolic's experience of his/her caregivers.

Patient: Both of us were sort of, I don't know how to describe it, the kind of state were in at the time, but . . . everything was just all messed up. So we got married, but then a friend of mine told me about this doctor in Mexico, so we went down there, and I got an abortion, and we came back and we sort of have been going along as if we aren't married at all. Now the school I go to . . . we have jobs. Six weeks of the year we spend on jobs. Let's see, we went back to Detroit and lived together a couple of months, and he went back to school. And I owe the school of whole lot of money because I didn't go on this overseas thing, and they are charging me for that.

Apparently she breached a contract with her school. An intuitive or intuitive symbolic is likely to break a contract. Until this point one might still think Ms. J is an intuitive character who is impulsive, tends to use rationalization and denial, and is somewhat irresponsible, although we also have hints of symbolic factors.

Patient: I really didn't want to have anything to do with school or anything. I wasn't coming back. So I decided to stay in Detroit and work and he went to school and a couple of weeks after, he came back to get me, and I really didn't know how to feel about that. I didn't think I was feeling anything and I told him I couldn't. But then the next week I got what I think was the afterbirth of when I had the abortion, because they really didn't take care of me and I didn't know what it was, and I just sort of panicked. I called him and he came and got me, and he took me back to school with him. I made some very superficial arrangements with the administration to keep going to school, but I didn't start taking classes or anything. I got a job in town. Then in the winter, both of us went to Washington to work. And it was sort of . . . we just spent all our time playing kids games, and drinking, and not really coming around to what was going on at all. When it was time to go back to school, I just couldn't go back. I don't know why or what it was that was bothering me or anything. Then I stayed in Washington for 3 more months after that. And I lived in sort of a student boarding house, which I think is about the only thing that really kept me going. The whole social situation in the city, I was in. That was getting to me. Martin Luther King died. That really hit me, completely disproportionately. And then when Kennedy died, I went to the funeral, and I got really flipped out on the idea of dying.

As she speaks it sounds as if the feelings about death and dying overtake her. Feeling washed-over by affect is a symbolic characteristic, although it may also fit an intuitive.

Patient: I got really scared and I wanted to go back to school, not because I wanted to go back there so much, but because where I was, was just too much to take, and school was the only place that even seemed acceptable to me.

As she talks, she sounds needy and depressed, not whiny or strained, but with an empty, open-sore quality to her mood. This is more typical of a symbolic.

Patient: So I called my parents and got them to agree to pay whatever I couldn't get from financial aid through my school.

Her parents helped her. But we must recall she was their cute, smart girl who was to bring credit to them. Their help could be help contingent on their needs being met, which often is a symbolic's parenting experience.

Patient: I called the school and they let me back in. When I went back I couldn't buy a tube of toothpaste. I got the feeling from my boyfriend that he just didn't really want me around at all and I was really pinning a lot of my hopes on him. I stayed there in the summer, and then in the fall I went to another job in Phoenix. I lived with a group of people who I think were really good for me, cause they just kept me so busy that I didn't, they wouldn't let me, you know, be left around to myself somewhere. I didn't do anything. Everything was just sort of a whirl of activity. It really got me out of the state that I had been in in the summer.

Activity as an antidote for depression. Not a specific for any character structure.

Patient: Then I got an opportunity at that job to work longer. And I thought at the time it was okay for me to stay there longer and not go back to school. But now that I look back I think that the reason that I just took it was because I just still didn't want to go back to school. I never seem to make any progress there. It just has all these bad memories and associations.

She describes the impact a setting has on her. This supports a symbolic diagnosis.

Patient: So I worked for 3 months in the fall, and then I went back to Detroit and worked there another month in the winter, which cut into my studying time. When I went back there [to school], after that I just completely neglected to get into any academics or anything.

It is as if she is "sucked" into depression. Affects may wash over symbolics, who are often not well-defended.

Patient: Like, I just sort of superficially went through it and let everything fall through. I wasn't getting anywhere at all. And then I came here to work, which I'm doing now and I was doing, I felt like, really well. I don't let these things bother me, but I felt that if I was able to keep moving in other directions, I could take care of them sometimes [later]. Well, that was just going fine.

She is a bit too open in her use of action as a coping mechanism. An intuitive character would disguise matters for himself or at least for the interviewer, who is a stranger.

Patient: But now, like this boyfriend of mine has come out here.

The precipitating event.

Patient: And we get along much better. But we both have a hard time doing what it is that we're doing now. [We are] just letting all this other stuff snow us under. So that's where I am right now. For the past couple of weeks all this stuff has come back.

The bad memories of her boyfriend, the setting at school, and Kennedy's death all overtake her. She is clearly both intuitive and symbolic.

Patient: I feel that I can control myself enough so that I don't . . . it's not stopping me from functioning. I don't feel like I'm in any kind of emergency state.

This is denial. It is probable that she will be in an emergency state if not helped.

Patient: But I really feel that I should be, uhm, start working on some of the stuff so that I'm able to go back to school in the fall and really work and not try to avoid, just getting out there, or getting into it. [lengthy pause]
Therapist: You say that you feel that you should really start working on some of these things?
Patient: Yes, it's not just because I reached a decision. But now, with his presence and the presence of some of his friends, I hear things that I've sort of been able to . . . well . . . that I haven't had to confront in the last couple of months. I'm having to confront now. And I really think that I need some help now in really understanding what went on cause . . . when I look back I just completely felt rejected, by everyone, when I really had a problem and wasn't able to show in my former good style that I just got it from everyone.

She says she needs understanding. She probably means help to sort out the morass she is in, and recognition of who she is or what she is experiencing when she is not the person she feels she is supposed to be. She sounds forlorn.

Patient: And it makes me feel really resentful to a lot of people. And I can't talk to my parents, except on a kind of basis that just doesn't have any meaning. As long as we don't get into anything deep it's okay.

You can't talk to them at all?

Patient: I don't really think I ever could, and I sort of, I don't know, I have the feeling that I'm the one who's looking out for their welfare, that I'm the one who's careful not to say anything that's going to get either one of them upset or worried or anything.

Role reversal is evidence of symbolic parenting experience.

Patient: Like, when I was in high school, periodically I'd go into this thing. Like, I was worried about dying. Well, I . . . this first came to me when I was in my junior year of high school. And it got my mother so upset, she kept saying, "Well, is it problems with boys?" Or she was just completely not seeing it at all. And it got her upset that it made me feel bad to even express to her which I soon thereafter ceased to do.

It was not that her mother was not sufficiently concerned. Ms. J realized that her mother was so upset that Ms. J had to stop revealing her inner experiences.

Patient: And whenever I even mentioned it to my father, it was sort of on a subversive basis, so that she [her mother] wouldn't have to get all upset that something was wrong with me. [Pause ½ minute]

An unusual use of the word "subversive." For her mother's sake Ms. J had to have no defects.

Patient: I just really have no idea that anything was even wrong with me. The farther away I get from it the more able I am to see it.

Here is a clue as to how to approach treatment. The therapist must help her to get some distance from her problems in order for her to get understanding. She uses distance (sometimes through moving) to cope, just as Ms. L used thinking as a coping device.

Patient: I just feel like I am at the point where, if I can get some help, that would make it easier for me. The thing now is that . . . that I wanted at least practically speaking to . . . to be able to go to school next year. I'm way behind on the amount of credits and whatever else I need. It doesn't bother me so much, the fact that I'm beginning to realize that I really don't want to go back. I only have a year there. I feel like adjusting these things enough in my mind so I can face it and the people. And I get really . . . I just completely clam up around people from school. And I felt in some ways like I haven't had any real friends, that I've been so attached to this one person that everything I've said and done these last years has just completely circled around him.

"Attached" and "circled" are a symbolic's words.

Patient: And I sort of isolated myself from the rest of the world. And when he's around I always slip into that, though I don't feel it as much. It might be. And I'm really possessive. Everything else falls behind. I'm really possessive. I feel like I'm possessive of his time and demanding and that I'm just really not enough of my own person.

She is describing a symbiosis into which she slides. Symbiotic merger is pathognomonic for symbolic character structure. Identify of self and direction are impaired.

Patient: I'm majoring in elementary, but I have no idea in my own mind, if that's anywhere near what I want to do. And I just went to college, because, you know, I thought everybody went to college. Like my parents are very happy that I want to be a teacher. I don't know if I want to be a teacher or anything. There is a lot of things I just like to try to do, that I've always been afraid to, to do some things. I would be starting at the level of someone who's in first grade, things in art and stuff and just lots of stuff like that. And I want to be able to ah . . . just feel that I can do those things and not feel I'm not doing things for myself.

A problem with identity, and probably feelings of deprivation as well. Undifferentiation of self appears in relation to direction, not to function (as distinct from the operational).

Patient: That there are things I'm not doing because other people would disapprove. [Pause] I don't feel that, right this minute. Sometimes when I talk about what's happened to me a couple of years ago, I feel like it's happening all over again. It's just physically . . . it's just the most horrible feeling.

She is overtaken by the memory and affect. Identity diffusion.

Therapist: Physically?

Patient: And mentally as well, yeah . . . and last summer too I just couldn't bring myself to talk to other people. I couldn't. I felt that I was getting a whole lot of rejection from this guy, who I felt like I followed through with him, when he needed me. And when he didn't anymore it was "so long" to me . . . and I really had a lot of bad feelings for him in that way. Uhm . . . when I went to Detroit . . . then he came out here to work. I slept with a couple other boys. I told him, just to make him angry. And I really felt like he deserved it. And it was very hard for me to see that I was doing anything wrong by treating it the way I did in terms of him. And even though I do things, I feel like I get so much pressure from him, to listen to him, to do the sorts of things that he wants . . . me to do.

An issue of control. Control is a common concern of an operational. Here control probably is involved in self-definition.

Patient: Like he started seeing a therapist at school. And I was even resisting, I think, doing the same thing, just because I know that he wanted me to do that. [Pause ½ minute.] I tend to become really attached to specific individuals and center anything I do around them.

"Attached" and "center."

Patient: Since I came out here this spring there was another boy, who I just have been spending all my time with, who lives where I do and works where I do. I know that I just shouldn't confine myself in that way. But I don't know what it is at all. But I tend to attach onto just individual persons and not really do a lot of reaching out. And I really feel I should be doing that, reaching out.

Therapist: You do?

The therapist is pushing her to reach out.

Patient: Yeah, because otherwise I put so much of myself into someone else, there isn't any of me really. And it isn't a very positive thing. I really get demanding of other people, of that person's time and what they want to do, which is really completely up to them. Then I get resentful, because they are taking some of my time, which I am giving anyhow. [Pause ½ minute.]

She describes the loss of identity inherent in her symbiosis, its deleterious effects on her and her partner, but her feeling of being lost when she is without an attachment.

Patient: I feel like from my background I just got into a kind of environment where I didn't have any other skills or reactions to handle the things that are happening to me, all the moving around and just all these different jobs. I would get really a feeling at the beginning . . . of being lost, being afraid, being alone. I don't know if that's being so unreasonable.

Therapist: All the moving around you said?

Patient: Yeah, even when I came here when I was on the bus, cause I really didn't know anybody here that I would definitely be hooked up with, I sort of got panicky about the thought of not knowing anyone here.

"Hooked up with."

Therapist: This time you mean?

Patient: Yes. [Pause 1½ minutes.] Oh, I went through that . . . It sort of came across the other night that I had this feeling, these feelings where I think that I'm much better than just about everybody else. And in some ways that really starts to get me down. Well, I don't know, if it's a sign what's happening to me or if it's what happening that makes me sort of spiral backwards. Where I work, when I really feel like I'm doing my best is when I don't have these feelings.

And last summer when I couldn't even talk to anyone else
is when I really had these feelings . . . that I was so much
better than anyone else. So if that I could just find out what
that's about. The only thing that my boyfriend and I would
talk about when we were together is how much better we
were than anyone else.

Following the pause she describes feeling grandiose, perhaps
because she is unattended during the long pauses.

Therapist: Better?

Patient: Yes, and that the way we handled things was right, and
the way we thought about everything was right. [Short
pause.] And last summer it was hard for me. I felt that
when I was around him and other people, that he didn't
want other people to know that we were related in any
way, especially other girls. I took that really hard. And yet I
couldn't cut myself off from him, because I felt that he was
the only person that I really had. [Pause ½ minute.]

A very pathetic quality to her voice, manifesting intense affect.

Patient: And another thing like . . . I felt a lot of resentment for
my parents in the last couple of years and just haven't . . .

Therapist: A lot of resentment toward them?

Patient: Yeah, for a whole lot of things. I don't know how justified some of them are. I've also felt a lot of resentment
toward my boyfriend's mother. And I've always felt that
she's been working against me. And . . . well . . . in some
ways she has, because she wants his attention. That was
her only bind—I think as much as I want his attention—
maybe even more so. And uhm . . . let's see, about 4
months ago, she arranged for him through a lawyer of hers
to get a divorce, which we're doing now. It will be, I guess,
something settled next Monday or something.

The divorce is a likely reason why she applies for treatment
now. This is of interest because it is only the symbol that is
changing. In effect, she has been divorced all along.

Patient: I don't know, cause we just never lived together, like we
were married or anything. And I haven't even used his
name or anything. I have just always signed that I was

single but I think in some ways that I'm really resentful towards him now. His marrying me at the time, and I told him then that I thought that I would feel that way someday. And I think that it's hard for him to understand that. Though I don't really know cause he's been . . . I haven't seen him for such a long time and he was in a lot of therapy. But it's really hard for me now even to treat him as though nothing's changed with him. And that he's acting differently. And it's hard for him too.

Therapist: He is acting differently now?

Patient: Yeah, but I still have this completely whole picture in my mind, all these facades of reacting to him. But at least now I feel like I know when I'm being sarcastic. Whereas before I thought I was just being . . . [One minute pause.]

Her inability to recognize when she is sarcastic is more confusion than it is isolation of affect as we would expect in an operational or an operational symbolic.

Patient: The day when I called in, I felt really eager to talk, but this morning when I woke up I almost felt like nothing was wrong with me. And I really didn't need to come here, and I sort of had to sit at home and think about that I did need to do it. I really feel that a kind of resistance in me is taking me this long even to do something about it.

Therapist: You do feel it even now?

Patient: I get into situations where all of a sudden these feelings come over me.

Notice her phraseology—"These feelings come over me." She is overcome. We have evidence for all these intuitive characteristics and now for the symbolic ones. She is clearly an intuitive symbolic.

Patient: And I start treating things disproportionately, like I used to last year. I feel that a lot of the time, though I can really be in the present, but I'm in the past, even so that it isn't helping me. And I know when I go back to school with all that, everything from the past being there, but it's really hard for me to go ahead with all the old people I know.

No time barrier, a dedifferentiation of time. This is more a loss of definition than it is the inability to take into account history or the future, which we would encounter in the pure intuitive.

Patient: And the whole thing, coming out here and just not really knowing anyone with whom I used to associate makes it a lot easier. But I'm afraid that I'm really easily seduced into doing things the way that I'm used to. The ways that make me feel badly, when I go back to school and when I see the people who I knew from several years, instead of the people I just know for a couple of months.

Again she describes being responsive to the surroundings. Distance and new associates help.

Patient: And I feel like even with people that I just met that I have to well . . . especially at the beginning of the summer I felt that I had to really grab a hold of myself and not let myself be suspicious of other people or resentful or anything like that, because these feelings were popping up where they shouldn't have.

She lacks the ability to separate objects. She is aware that she is suspicious and resentful of people who have not disappointed her.

Patient: I thought that everybody was going to. I just wasn't trusting and I really have had to, I feel, sort of just use willpower. Well, this isn't how it really was and I shouldn't be using my bad feelings on people I don't even know.

She has too much insight. She lacks defenses.

Patient: [One minute pause.] One thing I started to associate with this boy, whose name is Sheldon, is that when he's around at times I start having these old feelings of being afraid to die. And since he's come I got it a couple of times. I think that I have it pretty much under control. I know that if it starts to well up, it gets over me so that I can't sleep or either I eat so little or I eat so much.

She describes being washed over with affect. A very forlorn quality to her voice.

Patient: And it just starts to cave in on everything that I'm doing or trying to do, and I just get so caught up in it and it won't go out of my mind. And that's one thing that I had a lot of last summer. That's why I ran back to school, cause I thought that at least I had something to hold onto there. [Pause 1½ minutes.] And my friend, Sheldon, right now said that he wants to start spending a lot of time with me again, because I'm just so afraid that he's going to do me in and that I just can't go in for that sort of thing again. Yet on the other hand as soon as I feel bad, I feel like calling him up and talking to him.

She has trouble titrating the attachment.

Patient: So it's just not very satisfactory, cause I still . . . I'm just so much treating him in the ways things used to be where he's out to get me, where I still have to depend on him to talk to me, or to take me places. Uhm. [Pause.] And that's something that's going on right now. It isn't so serious . . .

Denial.

Patient: . . . because if we both try hard we can for short periods of time do what's going on now, but otherwise we can just so easily slip into this . . . this old thing which is like a power struggle and wanting to make the other person feel inferior and worthless. [Short pause.] And if I'm really good, I can take a lot of that and put out a lot of support, but then I start feeling really shaky about what I'm doing and, uhm, quivery inside, afraid to do it.

It is not quite clear whether enhanced self-esteem or sense of direction makes her less vulnerable, but they probably link together. Another clue for treatment.

Therapist: Some of the time?
Patient: Yeah, and I, a little bit, have those kind of feelings with everyone. So that I just can't completely put out without being afraid of being taken or being taken advantage of . . .

Ms. J's attachment and identity issues are obvious. Even her relationship to her caregiver suggests role reversal, with a narcissistic component to the parent's part. We should not be surprised that Ms. J also has intuitive qualities and few operational ones: she is an intuitive symbolic.

In contrast to an intuitive character, Ms. J's uses of projection, denial, rationalization, and action were not facile. She failed to fulfill an obligation to her school, but made no effort to project responsibility onto the school or to conceal her own irresponsibility. Even at the outset, Ms. J did not conceal from herself or from the therapist her affective state during adolescence when she was frightened of dying.

When she finished stating her presenting problem, Ms. J said that she should start working on some things now. However, she then stopped talking: she was asking the therapist to do the work at that point. We construct this because, when the therapist echoed Ms. J's statement that she felt she should start working on things, she spoke of people not helping and then talked about feelings of rejection and resentment toward her parents for not taking better care of her. The patient in her first interview expected the therapist to be a good parent substitute (although clearly the patient was also working, i.e., presenting a picture of herself and her problems).

Chapter 7

THE DIAGNOSTIC PROBLEM
PRESENTED BY DEVELOPMENT
OF FORMAL OPERATIONS

In this chapter we will discuss a complication in the system, which can cause difficulties in diagnosis. This complication may turn diagnosis into a judgment call about which even the persons most sophisticated in applying our system may disagree. This complication is the formal operational correction. We believe that formal operational corrections are the final modifiers to character structure, to social cognition (Malerstein & Ahern, 1982), just as they are to physical cognition.

In the formal operational period the adolescent uses hypothetico–deductive reasoning—thinking about thinking. For example, he considers many possibilities when trying to understand what governs the oscillation frequency of a pendulum.

In parallel fashion, an operational character wonders if it is always best to tell the truth. He is then moralizing about moralizing, a form of thinking about thinking. An intuitive character's formal operational correction may be enlightened self-interest. He may learn that it is best to see his customer's interest in order to make a sale. The rigid obsessional traits of an operational symbolic character, which help him to define himself and to separate himself from another, may be softened by a formal operational correction in the form of a conscious recognition that bad characteristics come in degrees. An intuitive symbolic, who maintains through acquisition of narcissistic supplies his sense of self as good and as distinct from bad persons, by recognizing his tendency to see the part as the whole may at times be able to see himself as good, even when he has been criticized or when he fails at a particular endeavor. He may do this by saying to himself, "That is only part of me, not all of me," adding a formal operational correction. He may also do this by finding another narcissistic gratification, adding or substituting another intuitive correction, e.g., pointing out that it was another's fault.

This use of formal operational correctives, i.e., thinking about thinking or second order processing, leads the diagnostician to ask himself, what does the patient really want (i.e., what is his basic investment), and how does the patient basically process information? If the patient is correcting for something, then for what? These kinds of questions are not new to dynamic psychotherapists. They require the kind of judgment that therapists exercise when using any model that accepts unconscious motivations as important. One tries to identify the underlying theme, to see what really "runs the show." An experienced therapist can usually decide what is "cake" and what is "frosting," but not always. Ms. J's diagnosis was easier than most others, as she had few formal operational corrections to her intuitive symbolic attributes.

Aside from providing diagnostic problems, formal operational corrections are of special importance to treatment. We think that, although expression of character structure may be modified, in adults character type is not changeable. Treatment of character structure problems primarily consists of changing through formal operational corrections the expression of character structure, or of modifying rigid formal operational corrections already constructed by the patient.

Part III

TREATMENT

Chapter 8

STANCE AND CONTEXT

For psychoanalysis Freud (1959a) recommended the pure abstinent stance, not only to allow for transference interpretation but also because he regarded the state of nongratification as motivating. Since Freud, the significance of the psychoanalytic situation or relationship has been addressed repeatedly in literature on the theory of therapy. Ongoing debate has centered around whether the psychoanalytic setting should be one flexible enough to accommodate patients who might not be able to tolerate the privations of the pure atmosphere recommended by Freud. The debate includes arguments both that psychoanalysis is indicated for almost anyone (Volkan, 1976) and that only certain persons are able to benefit from psychoanalysis (Freud, 1959a; Brenner, 1979), as well as dispute over how much of a deviation in method disqualifies the treatment as psychoanalysis (Eissler, 1953; Gill, 1954; Greenacre, 1954). Other arguments concern who sets the psychoanalytic frame (Langs & Stone, 1980), whether the analyst is responding to the unconscious expectations of the patient when the analyst takes an abstinent stance, whether even the good analysand may require more flexibility than that offered by the pure abstinent atmosphere, and whether the

pure abstinent stance is inherently miserable for the analysand (Brenner, 1979; Greenson, 1978).

We differentiate stance from context. Stance is the
abiding approach taken by the therapist, whereas context
is the patient's experience of the therapist's approach. Together stance and context make up the psychotherapeutic
relationship.

We regard the abstinent stance as not helpful for the
symbolic or the intuitive, but preferred for the operational
character, who essentially is the good analysand. The goal
is insight, and the major techniques used are clarification
and interpretation—ultimately transference interpretation. In this type of case a protective or parental context
confounds the technique and undermines the goal. A non-
abstinent, interactive stance creates difficulty knowing
when the patient's behavior stems primarily from himself
rather than from the therapist or their relationship. Caretaking may send a message that the therapist cares about
and will take care of the patient, or that the patient needs
to be taken care of. A caretaking stance tends to "contami-
nate" the transference, making its analysis problematic.

A pure abstinent stance is a fiction. But in its purest
form it sends the most ambiguous message possible.
When the therapist takes an ordinary social stance he
gives the patient a good deal of information, and cues the
patient to respond in terms of a particular social frame.
Thus less of the patient's construction of the therapist
comes from within the patient.

We instruct our students to start with an abstinent
stance and to watch for signs of how the patient experiences such an ambiguous setting. In this way a beginning
assessment of the patient's character and of some transference issues may be made. We know different things
about a patient depending on whether he responds to the
abstinent stance as a safe situation, a deprivation, a gratification, a test, or an invitation to merge. If he feels the

therapist as abandoning him, he may feel lost. If the therapist is attentive to how he is experienced by the patient, i.e., to the context, the therapist will better understand what stance to take and how to work with the patient, what techniques to employ, and what goals to set.

The following case of Ms. D and the positions taken by the discussants illustrate how understandings may differ among therapists, and how such understandings may lead to different recommendations for treatment as well as different assessments of the results of treatment. We identify Ms. D as a symbolic character. This identification of course influences our understanding of the context, and our corresponding recommendations.

The primary issue in the case presentation of Ms. D was why she was terminating treatment. Planning to leave the city where her therapist was located, Ms. D refused all efforts on the part of her current therapist to find her a new therapist with whom to continue treatment in her new location. Two different explanations were advanced by discussants: (1) Ms. D was fleeing treatment because of intolerable and undealt-with feelings she experienced in the treatment situation, and (2) the patient's experience was not one of termination, but merely of an extension of her continuing attachment to the therapist.

Ms. D, a 30-year-old single woman, began seeing her therapist before she was admitted to the hospital with paranoid symptoms that followed an involuntary job transfer. She had been hospitalized 7 years earlier for similar symptoms after she had finished graduate school. She had been treated with medication for both episodes. During the later hospitalization she was told by the ward physician, not her own therapist, that she was "vulnerable to stress." Subsequently, during an additional 1½-year course of outpatient therapy, she had two additional paranoid episodes that remitted with the same medication in substantial dosage, but that required no hospitalization.

Little background history was given in discussion of
Ms. D. She was the only child of parents who were very
different from each other. Her father was from a prestigious urban family who disapproved of his marriage to
her mother, a lower-class country girl. Ms. D's father, a
prominent business leader, had high expectations for her
as he had for himself: he sent her to the best schools,
where she did well, and he expected her to achieve in the
corporate world and she did. Ms. D identified with her
father and his family and was embarrassed that her mother came from a poor farming family. She was also humiliated by her mother's frequent hysterical outbursts, inability to tolerate stress, and 2 periods of psychiatric
hospitalization.

Much of the content of the patient's psychotherapy
involved the patient's conflicts about her father, i.e., her
wanting his approval on the one hand and her resenting
his controlling her on the other, and about the vicissitudes
of her job. Although she came for her therapy sessions
regularly, she did not appear to have any personal feelings
toward the therapist. The patient originally viewed her
various psychotic episodes as being caused by a chronic
glandular condition for which she was also being treated.
Eventually she separated her physical condition somewhat from her psychiatric illness and attributed her break-
downs to her "vulnerability to stress." This explanation
was substantially correct, but it was also a catch phrase
that operated as a part identity: her denial (and externalization) shifted from the glands to the phrase. Her major defense, denial, remained intact during therapy, and
the therapist did not appear to be trying to undermine it,
nor in our opinion should the therapist have done so.

As therapy progressed Ms. D gained some psychological distance from her father and his expectations and considered what her own goals might be. She became more
dissatisfied with her work. Although her job was prestigious, she felt humiliated and resented its more menial

aspects, such as buying a birthday gift for her employer's wife. Her attitude apparently became obvious, and when her boss commented about her resentment, she felt humiliated and left her job. After leaving, she applied herself to discovering what she wanted to do with her life. She took a battery of tests that indicated that she would like and would excel at a job in administration, for which she had the training and experience, but that she would be more satisfied performing this work in some setting other than the corporate world. To Ms. D the corporate world was equivalent to urban life, high stress, and high expectation—everything for which her father stood.

She searched for a job across the country and eventually found one she wanted in a small town not far from where her mother had grown up and where many of her mother's relatives whom she had always found to be kind and gentle still lived. She also felt she would be better off outside the city because of her "vulnerability to stress."

The therapist thought it was very important for this patient to continue therapy in her new location, or at least to have the name of a therapist in case of another decompensation. Ms. D, however, denied that there would be any future problems because she was removing herself from her father's domain (with some degree of approval from him) and from the stress of the city. Her other reason for not accepting a referral was that, in her new location "people thought anyone who saw a therapist was crazy." Furthermore, there was no way to keep people from knowing she saw a therapist because it was "a small town where everyone knew what everyone else was doing." Finally, there "would not be a female therapist" (the current therapist was female) "and a male therapist would not understand" her. Nevertheless her therapist located two therapists in Ms. D's town and two more in adjacent towns, so that the patient would at least have their names in case of a crisis.

With only a few weeks of therapy remaining, the therapist became concerned because Ms. D refused to go through "the termination process." Although the patient acknowledged that she would miss the climate where she was now living and that she had "gotten a lot out of therapy," she denied having any problem in giving up the therapist or that she would miss the therapist. The therapist felt sure Ms. D would leave therapy with her feelings relating to separation from the therapist "undealt with."

One of the discussants wished to focus on the "real reason" why the patient was leaving. He pointed out that Ms. D was subject to feelings of humiliation, that she was embarrassed by her mother's lower-class status, hysterical outbursts, and psychiatric hospitalizations, and by having to do "menial" tasks. She had left her job because of being humiliated. He proposed that she was now leaving therapy because being in therapy implied a defect, and that it was humiliating for her to consider herself in any way defective. He reminded the conference members that throughout therapy Ms. D maintained a steady denial that anything was really wrong with her. He argued that her denial of the need for psychotherapy and her subsequent resistance to a referral should be used to interpret her feelings of humiliation about having psychological problems. This interpretation would be offered with the hope of helping the patient to begin to make a connection between her feelings, her behavior, and her symptoms, and to lessen to some degree the rigidity of her denial. This clinician was committed to a psychoanalytic framework and typically took an abstinent stance toward his patients. Perhaps he construed the stance of the presenting therapist as abstinent.

Although this patient is particularly vulnerable to humiliation, we saw no evidence that she experienced her psychotherapy as humiliating. Perhaps if an abstinent stance had been taken she would have felt humiliated. In fact, the presenting therapist took a parental or nurturant stance as demonstrated by her concern during Ms. D's hospitalization, her close monitoring of the medication, and her efforts to find a therapist for Ms. D in her new community, and by the personal warmth of this particular therapist. Furthermore, we propose that when the patient leaves she will not regard the relationship as ended. We postulate that her resistance to a referral and unwillingness to say goodbye actually represented her need *not* to terminate, but to carry the therapist with her: she did not want to replace the therapist because she did not plan to lose her.

One of the conference participants suggested that perhaps the relationship with the therapist had been experienced as mothering, and that, on some level, Ms. D recognized that a mothering environment—symbolized for her by the rural community—was healthier for her than a fathering environment—symbolized by the city. Ms. D had taken her particular experience with her female therapist and had generalized its healing power to a greater mother, the rural environment, specifically the rural environment of her own mother and where her mother's relatives still lived. Finally, another conference participant suggested that complete separation/termination from the therapist was not necessary and that there might be occasional telephone calls.

These latter two suggestions coincide with our own method of understanding and treating a symbolic patient. We might have recommended a therapeutic stance that allowed the patient to attach, as Ms. D in fact did and from which, in our opinion, she benefited. We might also have recommended that Ms. D be allowed to continue the attachment in attenuated form, perhaps by writing to the therapist or at least by the therapist not insisting that she go through a termination process.

We do not, however, dismiss the suggestion of the clinician who recommended a more abstinent stance. We think if the abstinent stance were taken with Ms. D early in therapy by a skilled therapist who *also* would allow the patient to experience attachment, then any feeling of humiliation experienced by Ms. D regarding therapy might have been worked through. In time, perhaps more mature defenses might have been substituted for or added to her denial defense. The goal would have been for her to develop a more facile or diversified defensive system against future breakdown, and for her to become acquainted with and acquire some degree of mastery over her denial. Reaching such a goal might take a long time. Perhaps such an approach would have more far-reaching effects than a nurturant stance. On the other hand, if the therapist who took a more abstinent stance was not very skillful, Ms. D might have fled treatment much earlier or might have decompensated again, thus requiring rehospitalization.

In treatment an agent of change corresponds to a particular psychological mechanism of change. For example, interpretation, an agent of change, is intended to assist a patient's understanding or insight, a mechanism of change. Likewise suggestion is intended to help a patient choose a direction. As psychotherapists know, however, their is no one-to-one correspondence between the intent of a therapist and the intervention of the effect on the patient. Interpretation results sometimes in defensive build-up, sometimes in a sense of being cared for, and sometimes in feeling criticized with attendant humiliation or outrage. Similarly suggestion may stimulate revolt or stagnation, or may have no effect at all.

If the most abiding characteristics of a person are his style of social cognition and his basic social investment and if these characteristics are firmly established sometime after age 7 or 8 as a particular way of experiencing and being in the world, then it follows that such a person who has constructed a particular style of social cognition and investment will consciously and unconsciously use any psychotherapeutic stance differently than a person who has constructed one of the other styles of social cognition and basic investment. Hence when a psychotherapist uses an overall treatment approach he should be aware of the social cognition and basic investment that define the character structure of his patient.

Although there usually is a correspondence between the stance, i.e., the abiding approach taken by the therapist, and the therapeutic context, i.e., the abiding ambience as experienced by the patient, context may not correspond to stance. The stance presented by a therapist is communicative of social and emotional information that the patient will process as he does any other social and emotional information in terms of his own social cognitive style and basic investment, i.e., in terms of his character structure. The fewer clues the therapist gives about his attitude toward the patient, of course, the more the patient must rely on his own construction of the situation. Even when the therapist demonstrates a particular attitude, the patient may still construe that attitude as he usually experiences the attitudes of others, particularly others in authority.

Ms. A's and Mr. B's therapists took similar psychotherapeutic stances. The two patients made similar assumptions about their therapists. Each of the therapists drew attention to the assumptions of their patient. However, the two patients responded differently to the similar interventions of their therapists.

Ms. A, an operational character, was a 26-year old, single, unemployed clerical worker who sought treatment because of difficulty in choosing a career. She had recently been dismissed from two positions. She realized that in the first position she had tried to do things the way she thought they should be done rather than doing what she was told to do. The second dismissal, however, surprised her because it was from a "girl Friday" job where she thought functioning autonomously would be valued. Certain career opportunities were not open to Ms. A because she did not have a college degree. More oriented to function than to labels she had quit college 3 credits short of graduation, having decided "a degree was not necessary." She then left home to "go out on my own," but her parents telephoned every week to see how she was and tried to help by suggesting career possibilities and supporting those she proposed. Ms. A found herself unable to act upon either their suggestions or her own ideas. She brought up many of her ideas about possible careers with the therapist, who listened but offered no opinion.

One day Ms. A spoke of an interest in accounting. The following week she received a brochure in the mail about an accountant training program. At the next session, assuming that the therapist had responded to her mention of accounting by sending her the brochure, she thanked him. The therapist, who had been careful to maintain an abstinent stance, asked Ms. A why she thought he might have sent the brochure. In response, Ms. A recounted past and present examples of the continual involvement of her parents in her activities. She felt that her activities belonged to her parents—mother designing and making her costumes for school plays and father accompanying her during her riding lessons and reviewing her progress.

Ms. A then realized that she had transferred to her therapist the overprotective and controlling qualities of her parents. She also recognized that a major barrier for her in choosing a career was that in order to make an endeavor of her own, she had been seeking a career of which her parents would not approve. Each time her parents, however, approved of her ideas she then lost interest. She also discovered that she expected those in authority roles to have her best interests at heart just as her parents had. She had expected her bosses to have taken her good intentions into account and to have allowed her to function in ways that worked best for her.

Mr. B, a symbolic character, a 32-year-old, single man, complained of over-riding frustration and anger regarding the loss of the girlfriend to whom he had been attached for the past 5 years. His girlfriend left him because of his increasing possessiveness and restrictiveness. His father, whom he described as cold and unloving, had died 2 years previously. Although Mr. B said he experienced no feeling of loss after his father's death, he had begun at that time to cling more tightly to his girlfriend.

Denying loss by devaluing the lost person was characteristic of Mr. B. He described his mother, who died when he was 10 years old, as unloving, frustrating, and controlling. After her death he returned to his grandmother, with whom he had stayed earlier during an extended illness and whom he described as warm, loving, and admiring. He remembered sitting by the fireplace conscious of his grandmother's quiet comforting presence in the room.

In treatment, Mr. B focused on his father's and mother's worthlessness and his girlfriend's badness. The therapist took an abstinent stance and listened in silence, a silence with which Mr. B seemed to feel quite comfortable. One day, upon entering the room, Mr. B thanked the therapist for positioning the ashtray in the exact location where he himself always placed it. Mr. B had assumed the therapist was taking care of him. Hoping to give him insight into his assumption, the therapist said, "You felt I purposely placed the ashtray just where you'd place it?" Mr. B apologized for his mistake, and began to talk about plans to move out of the city and about his interest in other modes of therapy. At the close of the session, he reprimanded the therapist for his cruelty in mentioning to him his "social blunder." Despite Mr. B's injured response to the interpretation, at the next and succeeding sessions the therapist brought up Mr. B's reactions to his statement and tried to analyze Mr. B's angry feelings toward the therapist. Mr. B soon left treatment.

In both of these cases the therapist took an abstinent

stance, and in both cases the patient perceived the therapist as a caregiver. In both cases the therapist made an attempt at a transference interpretation directed toward insight into unconscious conflict. The similarity ended there: Ms. A used the interpretive intervention as information, relating her expectations of the therapist to her remembered early experience with her mother and father. As therapy progressed, she realized that her expectations of authorities reflected her early experience with her parents, who were overprotective and controlling, but also devoted to her best interests. The therapist's intervention had the effect of which Freud (1943, p. 385) wrote: "The transference is overcome by showing the patient that his feelings do not originate in the current situation, and do not really concern the person of the physician, but that he is reproducing something that had happened to him long ago. In this way we require him to transform his *repetition* into *recollection*."

Mr. B, on the other hand, took the interpretation as a reprimand and became disengaged from the therapist, whom he eventually categorized together with his worthless parents and bad girlfriend. Before the interpretation he experienced the therapist's silence as a warm, loving, admiring presence. He felt a union with the therapist, as he had felt with his grandmother and with his girlfriend before she deserted him.

The therapist decides which stance to take based on his understanding of how his patient is likely to experience that stance. How the patient will experience a stance is largely determined by the patient's character structure. Keeping in mind the patient's investment and cognitive style will guide the therapist in regard to his stance and alert the therapist to the way the patient is likely to experience the context. The therapist is then prepared either to modify his behavior to remain with the appropriate stance, or to discuss the discrepancy between his intent and the patient's experience of his stance if the patient can benefit from/tolerate such a discussion.

Mr. B gave clues that the therapeutic approach had started to fail when he began to discuss plans for moving away and to consider other modes of therapy. With a prior definitive character diagnosis, even if the stance toward Mr. B had been abstinent up to this point, the therapist would be more alert to a likelihood of difficulty at some such point and would be ready to change his stance.

In the next three chapters we propose distinct approaches or methods for the treatment of each one of the three character structure types. Once we have chosen the therapeutic stance, the techniques, goals, and curative agents follow. Just as the same context is not suitable for all patients, neither are the same goals and the same techniques.

There are some therapists who use a behaviorist approach with all patients, others who always use a systems approach, and still others who consistently use an insight-oriented approach. This is particularly true of therapists whose training has emphasized a single approach or who usually treat patients of a single character structure and thus believe that the approach that is effective with that group of patients is generally applicable. They formulate the problem to be treated in accordance with their particular approach. A behaviorally oriented therapist may accept the patient's behavioral definition of the problem and set up a schedule for modifying the patient's behavior; a systems-oriented therapist may understand the patient's problem as a family interactional problem and suggest treating the whole family; whereas an insight-oriented therapist may attempt to convert a patient's externalized complaint into an internalized one, which he can then undertake to analyze.

Many method-centered therapists—some of the classical psychoanalysts, for example—are person-centered as well. They modify their interventions according to their moment-to-moment understanding of what is happening with their patients. The "evenly hovering attention" recommended by Freud (1959a, p. 324) tends to fit this practice. Some psychoanalytically oriented psychotherapists tend to arrive at differential approaches to patients depending on their understanding of the patient's personality organization, i.e., whether the problem a patient has represents unconscious conflict or ego defect. If the former, they incline toward an uncovering approach; if the latter, toward an ego-supportive or educative approach.

As noted earlier in this chapter, psychoanalytic theorists differed as to whether or not psychoanalysis as a method should be reserved for patients who have no ego defects. Some psychoanalytic theorists believed that "parameters" may be invoked, that the method may be abridged, but only to the extent that the abridgement itself may later be analyzed (Eissler, 1953) or partially analyzed (Stone in Langs & Stone, 1980). Others deviated further, introducing such concepts as the "therapeutic alliance" (Zetzel, 1956) and the "working alliance" (Greenson, 1978). Kernberg (1975) used an abstinent stance with narcissistic personalities but recommended ego-supportive methods with borderlines, at least early in treatment. Kohut (1977) attempted to redefine psychoanalysis even more radically in order to make it relevant to the treatment of narcissistic personalities. Later Kohut proposed that this type of approach is required for all patients, ranging from the good analysand to the borderline (Baker & Baker, 1987). We contend that in some instances, although the therapist assumed an abstinent stance, the patient may have experienced a protective context.

Our approaches bear some relationship to Alexander's (1948) corrective emotional experience. Having reconstructed how a past figure caused the patient's pathology, Alexander behaved as had the past figure or in a manner opposite to the past figure. Whereas Alexander's efforts were highly specific and tailored to offset a causal agent peculiar to the problems of a particular patient, we attempt to adjust our attitude and approach to types of persons. In addition, Alexander's focus was on the techniques (advice, guidance, and manipulation) used by the therapist, whereas we emphasize the patient's experience of the therapist. This experience is based on what the patient brings to the treatment situation and to a lesser extent on particular techniques employed by the therapist.

We think of our approach as tailoring ourselves to a patient's style so that we may communicate with him. (For some patients being in communication is curative in itself. For others, it is only the vehicle for treatment.) We use our understanding of the patient's style to decide what kind of solution is likely to work for him and what kind of effort (manipulation, suggestion, interpretation) on our part is likely to assist in such a solution. It is principally in the area of stance supporting the therapeutic context that our model of character structure provides us with most useful guidance.

Chapter 9

TREATMENT OF THE OPERATIONAL

After over a decade of using our diagnostic system, we still have difficulty differentiating the pure intuitive and the pure operational from the intuitive symbolic and operational symbolic, respectively. We do not see many pure intuitives or pure operationals in our practice. Often when we initially think a person is an intuitive or an operational, we find as he continues in treatment that he is either an intuitive symbolic or an operational symbolic.

Nevertheless we have treated several intuitives and operationals long enough to feel confident that they are distinct from symbolics. Even if there are only a few pure intuitives and pure operationals or if those we believe to be intuitives or operationals are all symbolics who are so specialized along intuitive or operational lines that any symbolic issues lack significance, the treatment approaches for the pure intuitive and pure operational merit discussion.

The operational character, given his basically autonomous social-ego, is the good analysand. (Over the past 30 years we have seen very few good analysands. Many of the analysands we have known and many of the patients cited in the literature as good analysands we would diagnose as operational symbolic.) Mr. S was one of these (Malerstein & Ahern, 1982), as was Ms. L in Chapter 6, Ms. A in Chapter 8, and Mr. M in this chapter. Psychoanalysis as a method exposes and even cultivates those structures of the analysand's social-ego that are nonautonomous. Another word for such nonautonomous structures is transference. Analysis of the transference, the essence of psychoanalysis, makes the analysand's social-ego more autonomous, as illustrated by the case of Ms. A.

Freud proposed that the superego was the outcome of the oedipal complex. Fearing castration by his father for having sexual desires directed toward his mother, the boy represses his desires and uses what he believes to be the prohibitions and ideals of his father to form a superego, the boy's moral code.

We proposed a different mechanism for superego formation (Malerstein & Ahern, 1982). A child who experiences his caregivers as looking out for his interests is provided with a model of social beings and with communications out of which he constructs a basically autonomous superego. As noted in Chapter 4 we now prefer to call it a social-ego, as we consider the differentiation of morality from convention to be only quantitative. The social-ego comprises what the child views as the rules and codes of his social world, and especially of his caregiver. We propose that he constructs these social values or attributes much as he constructs physical attributes. Oedipal wishes along with incest may be taboo and frightening in Western culture. Other cultures, with different family structures attuned to different environmental demands, need not subscribe to the same codes for children or adults. But in our culture, oedipal wishes are at the evil and dangerous end of a continuum of codes that extends through lesser evils all the way to conventions such as proper attire and dinner-table etiquette. Social-ego factors that distinguish

the operational character from other characters are the gradedness of his codes and their independence from any
current event, thing, or person including the self, and the
affect involved.

THE FRAME ARGUMENT IN PSYCHOANALYSIS

When we direct our attention to treatment of the operational character we may point to the vast literature of
psychoanalysis. Our principal concern, the therapeutic situation or frame (Langs & Stone, 1980), which we call the
stance and the context, has also been a major focus of
psychoanalysis, especially in recent years, as noted in
Chapter 8.

Among psychoanalytic theorists there has been an
ideological struggle regarding the appropriate therapeutic
stance, with Langs (Langs & Stone, 1980) at one extreme
emphasizing the abstinent stance, and Greenson (1978) at
the other, arguing the significance of the therapeutic alliance. Stone (Langs and Stone, 1980) and Zetzel (1956)
took somewhat intermediate positions. In a sense it is difficult to place Kohut (1977) in this argument. Either he
redefined psychoanalysis to accommodate a broader range
of patients or he proposed a more general theory of therapy encompassing two modes of healing—identifications
(including transferences) and improved defensive structures. We think he redefined psychoanalysis, because he
did not emphasize the analysis of the transference that
would be appropriate at least in the good analysand, our
operational character.

Langs (Langs & Stone, 1980) has contended that his
patients opt for the abstinent stance. This certainly was
true for one patient of ours, a young opera student, Ms. P,
who wanted to learn why she was so awkward on stage.
With one of her coaches she could really sing: she did not

have to monitor herself in the coaching session, but simply give her best performance. Her patrons and other teachers told her what to do and how she should dress. For her, conservative dress and jewelry were the "ultimate hypocrisy," yet she tried to comply. When she complied, her voice and movements were forced and mechanical, making her performance seem unfinished. As patients usually do, this operational patient was telling the therapist how to treat her; in this case the message was to take the stance the coach had taken, an abstinent one.

THE ABSTINENT STANCE

The abstinent stance is passive and permissive, the therapist neither stating nor implying criteria of right or wrong. It is non-self-disclosing and abstains from gratifying the patient's infantile wishes. This abstinent stance does not mean that the therapist may not show empathy or respect for the patient or that the therapist should be cold, but it does preclude manipulation, guidance, expressions of approval, or efforts to bolster the patient's self-esteem.[17] In taking this stance the therapist hopes that the patient will be the active agent, free to say anything that comes to his mind, the corollary being that anything the patient says is a proper subject for exploration and understanding.

In treatment of an operational, the abstinent stance fosters the patient's experience of the therapy as supporting his ability, responsibility, and entitlement to function under his own auspices. Any failure to experience that context is transference, which is interpreted at some point.

The kindly, interested, respectful therapist, hired as someone generally experienced in psychological and emotional matters to help understand and to clarify the problems the patient is experiencing, does well to keep his intrusions to a minimum. This stance supports the context in which the patient may "try his wings." This ambiguous, abstinent context is a fertile setting for development of the transference neurosis. The message is given that whatever occurs to the patient to say is relevant, while the eventual transference interpretations are not confounded by gratuitous interventions. Aside from the content of transference phenomena (castration fears, oedipal love, or the like), structurally, transference interpretation separates present object representation, i.e., the therapist, from past object representations and accordingly separates self-representation and object representations.

ANALYSIS OF TRANSFERENCE

At the most basic level, transference for any character structure is the blurring of boundaries between the quality of the therapist's caregiving and the patient's construct of past caregivers.

As the operational character is able to tolerate the deprivation of the abstinent context, so he is able to fantasize and have insight without becoming confused, and to tolerate the painful affects that may accompany fantasy or insight into unconscious content including transference phenomena. It should be understood, however, that our recommendation of the abstinent stance is not in order that privation drive the treatment, as suggested by Freud (1959b). The abstinent stance is chosen because it lends itself to analysis of transference.

In analysis of the transference an analysand may experience homosexual ambivalent wishes of penetration by the analyst-father, projected rage anticipated from authority figures, intense love for analyst-mother, and expectations of being taken care of by the father-analyst. These various types of content, i.e., schemes, constitute failures

in differentiation of attributes of different object representations—and accordingly undifferentiation between attributes of self and object. For example, when experiencing projected rage against the father-analyst who the
patient experiences as wanting to hold him back, the patient is not differentiating the attributes that distinguish
father and analyst. He is also not differentiating attributes
of self from analyst, since any construct the patient has of
his father is also part of himself, particularly those attributes of self that he originally projected onto his father
and that justified his rage.

From a structural point of view, any transference phe-
nomenon marks the lack of a boundary between past others and current others and therefore between the patient
and past others. The overriding effect of interpreting
transference, hence giving insight into this diffusion of
ego boundaries, is to separate the patient from past adults,
and to make the patient more autonomous.

In terms of content, transference phenomena—assumptions made by the patient about the therapist—most
often reflect the patient's experience with his primary
caregivers during his formative years. Since the operational's basic construct was that his primary caregiver was
invested in his best interest, he makes this same assumption about the therapist. He transfers his experience of
being protected and perhaps controlled by his parents
onto other authority figures, including the therapist. Insight into the transference makes the patient independent.

Mr. M, an operational character, a young man who
felt confused about whether he functioned under the auspices of others (including the therapist) or under his own
auspices, objected to paying for an appointment he had
missed when he was involved in an auto accident on his
way to a therapy session. Aside from arguing that missing
the session was not his fault, he contended that the analyst had more money than he and could more easily afford

the loss. Later in the hour the young man commented that under similar circumstances his father would have absorbed the expense. The therapist's interpretation "but I am not your father" provided insight into the fact that the patient had been casting the therapist in the role of caregiver. The patient had transferred onto the therapist his wish to continue being taken care of by a father who would be responsible for dealing with life's reverses. This insight laid the groundwork for the patient's understanding of his assumptions that those whom he considered to be in authority or who were more affluent would and should (like his father) look after poorer, less powerful persons, (like himself). In exchange he had assumed he should accept them, not himself, as adult and in charge. Those assumptions were the essence of his conflict about autonomy, and related to his fears of adult sexuality and his anxiety and guilt about competitive urges.

To us, the fundamental interpretation of transference is insight into an operational's expectation that the therapist along with others in powerful roles will look out for the less powerful. Interpretation of such expectations, and of the fear, disappointment, and resentment when such expectations are not fulfilled, is central to treatment of an operational in our opinion.

Much other useful work may be done in treatment while the therapist awaits the appropriate time for this interpretation. For example, an operational character with an obsessive–compulsive personality may find his function in his relationships with other people in his work or in his analysis is compromised by his vacillation in thought and actions, by his use of undoing. Gaining insight into this defense may allow him some freedom to choose whether or not to use it (Weiss, 1967). He may laugh at and deautomate somewhat his swinging back and forth between topics. He may come to understand that he feels competitive with or overly submissive to authorities, an insight that may give him more control over such feelings when they arise.

As a result of transference analysis the operational character may find out that some of his beliefs and values are based on unconsidered and false assumptions. Such insight may confuse him for a while and cause him to reevaluate these values and beliefs. We don't expect, however, to change the fundamental assumption that the big and strong will necessarily take care of or take charge of the oppressed, the helpless, and the small. Although the operational may change his beliefs and expectations in a specific instance, and may even be able to catch himself making the assumption at times, he will most likely not change his basic expectation. For example, if he believes that a chairman of a department necessarily has the best interests of the staff and the students at heart, and if he learns that a particular chairman does not, he will probably continue to think there is a problem with that particular department or its chairman, and to expect other department heads to meet his assumption.

Because a patient with an operational character structure typically presents with issues about function or control of function, including inhibition of function and confusion as to whom his function belongs, the patient will usually assume that he will not be allowed to function autonomously in treatment. When this assumption is operative, the therapist may interpret it.

Through analysis of this core assumption the patient comes to recognize that what interferes with his function is not the therapist but his own guilt and anxiety about autonomy and initiative, about feeling "grown up." The essential insights are that his therapist is not his caregiver and that he is not a child who needs to do what the therapist wishes (such as produce material for analysis) or to defy the therapist (for example, by not producing material). Rather he is a separate, responsible person, able and entitled to function under his own auspices. The revelation that the therapist, like others in authority, does not own the patient's function gives the patient the freedom to choose what he does and believes. From such understanding and insight into his part functions, e.g., his fear or wish for a passive role, he may gain a sense of mastery and some measure of control over these part functions.

Basic to the treatment of the operational character is the patient's experience with someone who does not want and cannot be tempted to protect or to control him. In keeping with the abstinent stance the therapist does not put himself forward as "the expert," nor as the lover or rival. Consistent with not being the "expert" he may simply call something to the attention of the patient and make only piecemeal interpretations, allowing the patient to generalize from the particular and to make his own interpretations whenever possible. The operational character usually does not need to have interpretations worked out for him, e.g., Ms. A in Chapter 8. In spelling out an interpretation for an operational character, the therapist risks undermining the patient's independent functioning, his autonomy and initiative, and his often tenuous sense of himself as adult. This does not mean that the therapist must never make interpretations or must ignore resistance. It simply means that interventions are best kept to a minimum.

Beginning treatment with instructions to the patient may undermine the abstinent atmosphere. Such instructions send the message that the therapist is in charge and will cure the patient if the patient follows instructions. Freud's (1959c) elaborate instructions (before he had fully conceptualized his technique) to the Rat Man sent such a message. With a symbolic or particularly with an intuitive this may be the message one wishes to impart, but not with an operational character.

The operational character is the appropriate patient for psychoanalysis because of his autonomous social-ego, but is it necessary for an operational character to have a traditional analysis with frequent visits, recumbent position, and so forth? Might a less intensive therapy suffice? Inducing a good analysand who has another agenda to stay in treatment because he might profit from a "complete" analysis confounds analysis of what we consider the basic transference, the confusion as to who owns the patient's function. [The psychoanalyst Ralph Greenson may have been such an analysand; regarding his training analysis as insufficient, Greenson said he "had one for them (the analytic institute) and then one for himself."] The goal of treatment of the operational character, as of other character structures, depends on the problem he presents, as well as on his character structure. Sometimes he comes to solve some specific problem, such as making a particular decision. Within a few sessions he may come to some resolution. Sometimes of course the nature of the problem is one that requires insight into unconscious motivations and cognitions and their genetic roots. Whether the treatment of the operational character is to be psychoanalysis or a brief form of insight-oriented treatment, an abstinent stance is appropriate in order not to undermine the adult functioning of the patient and in order not to gloss over the dependent functioning of the patient.

What is a reasonable endpoint? Those operational characters we know who had extended relatively orthodox analysis (or several analyses) feel it was helpful. They can think of some things that could have been handled a bit differently by the analysts. Those who had several analytic experiences may judge the quality of work of a particular analyst, the experience or insight that seemed to help most, and what about themselves and their circumstances seemed to matter to the analysis. Psychoanalysis does not make the analysand a new person except where the treatment goes astray: Anyone we know before analysis was recognizable after analysis. We think the reasonable endpoint must be somewhere between a state of mere symptomatic relief, in which the patient acquires no new tools to deal with life, and that fantasized state of complete and perfect analysis.

In the treatment of the operational character, the therapist may clarify and interpret the patient's defenses in order to allow unconscious constructs, including their genetic components, to become conscious and available for interpretation. We believe the same technique is not generally helpful in treating intuitive or symbolic characters. Typically an operational character is more likely to process insights as information.

In summary, we recommend as the appropriate method for treating an operational character, regardless of whether the treatment is extensive or limited, an approach that does not deny his ability, responsibility, and entitlement to function under his own auspices. The major transference interpretation is directed toward the patient's assumption that the therapist is or should be looking out for the patient's interests, or in a more exaggerated form, the assumption that the therapist is overprotective, controlling, too ambitious for the patient, or overly competitive. In order to prepare for this interpretation, the stance of the therapist is one of abstinence, anonymity, and passivity. Through interpretation of the transference to the therapist as parent, the patient comes to realize that his behavior with others, particularly those in authority, reflects his assumption that his function and concerns over his function belong to another.

We doubt that insight into this assumption is permanent; rather, it must occur over and over again and must be worked through as the patient continues to behave, perhaps to a decreasing extent, on the basis of the assumption. Thus, because it is in the nature of cognitive structures to generalize and repeat and because an operational character will "forget" those experiences in which

his assumptions about those in authority led to difficulty,
he will again find himself trusting someone whom he
should not trust or struggling with someone who he assumes wants to control him.

Chapter 10

TREATMENT OF THE INTUITIVE

In our treatment of the intuitive we mind the lessons from the literature on treatment of patients with behavior disorders (sociopaths, psychopaths, and delinquents), particularly Greenwald's (1974) work. Each intuitive lies somewhere on a continuum that extends from psychopaths to patients with moderate behavior disorders to normals whose behavior is well-controlled. Thought pattern and motivation are basically the same in all persons along this continuum, although the thought patterns and motivations typical of an intuitive are most striking in persons who have outright behavior disorders.

Meeting the intuitive patient where he is means understanding the world from the intuitive's perspective or, as Greenwald (1974) termed it, from the "inside." Greenwald, although writing about the psychopath, provides us with the basics for approaching any intuitive. Greenwald asserted that the treatment literature betrays a lack of empathy and understanding of the psychopath. He told of psychopathic patients who reported having gone from therapist to therapist, eventually leaving each as in time the therapist referred to the patient's lack of morality. Although these patients readily evoke this sort of response,

sponse, Greenwald cautions psychotherapists to resist it, especially early in psychotherapy when the essential task is to establish a working relationship with the patient. Lippman (1949) noted that delinquents, by long experience with adults, must have the ability to distinguish friends from enemies in order to be successful delinquents.

A patient who as a child was left to take care of his own psychological and sometimes physical needs (the usual early life experience of someone who develops a behavior disorder) knows not to trust a stranger. The therapist thus must prove himself consistently and repeatedly. The therapist who does not accept the patient and who is judgmental about the patient's behavior and narcissistic goals will in one way or another convey this sentiment to the patient.

As we discuss Greenwald's work the reader would do well to substitute "intuitive character" in place of psychopath. Greenwald (1974) viewed most psychopaths in psychotherapy as being inadequate manipulators. (The ones who can manipulate adequately are not likely to seek psychotherapy.) Because of this inadequacy they are often in some kind of trouble. Greenwald identifies one of the therapist's jobs as making these patients better manipulators. The therapist must teach them how to achieve their goals in socially acceptable ways. He advises a therapist to use his own personal psychopathy. For example, Greenwald may share with a patient some experience that demonstrates Greenwald's own use of manipulation. He shows psychopathic patients that he is better than they are at working the system. He reveals his own selfish, narcissistic needs, showing the patient that there are similarities between the two of them. He may tell such a patient that the fee should be paid because he, i.e., Greenwald, likes money. Psychopathic patients understand this attitude. He shows the psychopaths that the difference between himself and them is that he has learned how to get what he wants and that he can teach them to do the same.

We think this is the proper therapeutic stance to take with the intuitive or behavior-disordered, narcissistic patient, although the doing so may not be natural for the many psychotherapists. The therapist is to be an educator or avuncular guide, a counselor, someone who has "been there before." Many therapists who work well with sociopaths have a testy manner which is nonjudgmental. They give the patient the impression of being up to par with him, perhaps even a bit ahead of him. These therapists establish their "credentials." When commenting on the patient's selfish desires and deviousness these therapists may have a joking or lighthearted quality. The patient has not embraced the rules, so it is distancing, at best, to moralize. At the same time the therapist guards his own self-interests, a fact that does not elude the patient.

In attempting to coax a young sociopath in a mental hospital for criminals to attend school and participate in other therapeutic activities, a therapist queried the patient about his nonattendance at school: "How come? Oh, you were at baseball practice? Oh, that was a required activity? Oh, I see." The patient answered with one excuse or another. The therapist's questions were all posed with a light touch—kidding around. It finally became clear that his technique was inadequate in this instance, as the patient's rationalizations continued. The therapist was then forced to play a trump card. He said "It is up to you. I don't have time to chase after you, but"—showing that he would protect himself, and would work within the rules—"I'll have to chart your not going and that will have some effect on your eventual release." This same therapist also played one-on-one basketball with this patient and outdid him each time. While playing, the therapist coached the patient in how he, the patient, could notice the moves the therapist was making and possibly learn to outdo him. It is not a coincidence that certain group approaches—transactional analysis, encounter, Synanon—that have been successful in the treatment of behavior disorders have a gamelike aspect. At the least, emphasis on skill in playing a game minimizes humiliation of the kind occasioned by certain traditional approaches.

In our approach the therapist is a guide and a model. He demonstrates that he may have impulses and yet can control himself. He establishes a mode of communication and understanding. Intrinsic to this approach is a measure of distrust, the therapist being alert to the patient's selfishness as well as being careful to look out for his own interests. The relationship is often contractual, with bargaining and limit setting, and includes a kindly attitude taken toward the patient's (and other persons') narcissistic interests, but does not necessarily gratify these interests. The kindliness toward narcissistic needs may provide a model for the patient to incorporate, resulting in the patient's less severe condemnation of his own selfish desires. Behavior-disordered patients [like their counterpart intuitive-phase children (Piaget, 1965a)] tend to condemn rule breaking severely, and hence often must deny their own transgressions or project them onto others, at the same time stringently judging others who break the rules. It is not unusual to hear a prisoner (almost invariably intuitive or intuitive symbolic) say with venom, "You scumbag child molester" to a fellow inmate or "You sadistic bastard" to a prison guard. If an intuitive can take a more kindly attitude toward his own antisocial impulses he may feel more comfortable and less likely to project them. When he cannot assume such an attitude he may project his impulses and divert his condemnation toward a colleague and may even refuse to associate with him.

Over the course of treatment with Greenwald, psychopathic patients became curious about how Greenwald was able to "get away with it," since his behavior was so much like theirs. Some years ago Windholz (1957) stated that Aichorn had taken a very similar approach to delinquents. Aichorn would say, "So you got caught stealing this watch. Now if I were to steal a watch, this is what I would do. . . ." Windholz explained that the delinquents learned that it was acceptable to have such selfish, illegal impulses and that such impulses could be controlled. The delinquents noted that Aichorn had thoughts and feelings similar to their own and yet was not in jail, wore nice clothes, had a nice office, and appeared to be successful. Greenwald described a parallel case in which he pointed out to a pimp that he, Greenwald, also made money from prostitutes: he did so by treating them and writing a book about them, and was praised, not jailed, for his actions. According to Greenwald, a therapist who can stimulate curiosity about such successes is in a good position to show psychopathic patients the self-destructiveness of their methods (Greenwald, 1974). Greenwald's point was that, if they could see their methods as self-destructive rather than as immoral or bad for society, psychopaths might find sufficient incentive to change these methods, and then might listen to the lesson that he could teach them. Essentially he was proposing an intuitive, i.e., self-serving goal.

The goal was "to learn control" (p. 372). As part of his technique he told them not to smoke, not to socialize with other patients in the waiting room, not to use the bathroom before sessions. This approach is reminiscent of EST (as well as of anti-addiction approaches such as Alcoholics Anonymous and Synanon), enjoining "responsibility" through self-control. Greenwald recognized that his patients had not learned to postpone gratification, had not learned methods for getting what they wanted while staying out of trouble. He undertook to teach them such methods.

Greenwald warned that once a psychopathic patient establishes a good relationship with a therapist, he might stop paying the fee. Greenwald claimed that this derives from the patient's thinking that, since he likes the therapist and as he does not like many people, this is payment enough. The patient sees the therapy as a gift of love, not a service for a fee. Greenwald viewed nonpayment as a key test: if the therapist continues to treat such a patient without a fee, nothing therapeutic will occur, because the patient will believe that cheating the therapist out of his fee means he is smarter than the therapist, and the therapist will then not be able to help him. Greenwald recommended that every session be spent discussing the nonpayment of fee until the patient initiates payment again. This constant discussion might tilt the balance between anxiety produced in the patient by the discussion and his not wanting to pay. Greenwald argued against threatening to discontinue treatment if the fee is not paid within a specified time because the threat would give such a patient an opportunity to project his failure in therapy upon the therapist who rejected him.

Greenwald saw the issue of nonpayment as a test of strength, and believed that the patient must accept the therapist as being in charge in order to learn from him. We agree that this is often true for such a patient. Additionally, identification with the therapist may be facilitated by the patient's seeing the therapist as stronger than himself. One therapist who worked with prisoners deliberately set up contests of strength at the beginning of treatment. Depending on the particular patient, he might defeat him at chess, wrestling, or boxing. (He is by now something the worse for wear from the latter.) Certain patients seek to attack the therapist's weaknesses, even while hoping he will remain intact. They do not really intend to destroy him but rather to test his indestructibility. If the therapist passes the test, they become somewhat more trustful that he can help them.

Although we think there is virtue in winning the

struggle over the fee or in other tests of strength, we think the main issue is the contract. If the therapist is to qualify as a suitable guide, he must pass the test imposed by the particular contract with his patient. If fee is part of the contract, then the therapist must be someone who is able to protect his pocketbook, his own interests. Otherwise what kind of teacher or guide, i.e., what kind of model, is he anyway? He is just another victim or another person who has "bought into the system."

Greenwald's eventual goal was to convert behavior into verbal expression. He stated that after self-control is established, the next step is to facilitate verbal expression of both hostility and dependency needs.

An intuitive character typically has problems managing affect. A therapist may help him recognize and verbalize his feelings instead of acting upon them in a way that promotes trouble. The goal is to recognize angry feelings and talk about them, not to be rid of them. Encouraging the patient to talk about feelings may reduce the global quality of his affects. All this assists in establishing self-control. With patients who prefer action, however, focusing on feelings may increase impulsive action, because such patients may not make a clear distinction between feeling and acting. We encourage the patient to think or feel before he leaps, but may phrase our intervention in terms of action. That is, we talk with the patient about what he is going to do about something rather than how he thinks or feels about it. Patients who make little distinction between thinking, feeling, and doing may assume that permission to think or feel constitutes license to do whatever they feel like doing. With such patients, a therapist may be better advised to focus on what the patient does or what he has done or is going to do, rather than on feelings *per se*.

Central to Greenwald's approach is limit setting. We do not prescribe the same stringent constraints, i.e., instructing patients not to talk to other patients, and so on. Perhaps this is a mistake on our part, since such stringencies should be understandable to an intuitive [just as they are the medium of exchange of an intuitive-phase child (Piaget, 1965a)]. It seems certain that having the patient see that he can control himself and credit himself for control would be useful. We do encourage any efforts he may make to use control and to stay out of trouble, and we also do set limits.

Traditionally, social workers in public agencies have dealt with intuitive patients, sometimes very effectively. In a public agency, fee may or may not be part of the contract. Certain narcissistic patients cannot tolerate the notion they are being treated for a fee. The narcissistic blow that they are being treated for a fee is more than they can bear. They may improve only if they are treated without fee or for a fee they consider nominal. Perhaps these patients should be treated only in a no-fee institution or clinic, since a therapist in private practice who expects a fee is likely to feel cheated if he works without one, even if no fee is required for the patient's improvement.

Since the characteristic cognitive style of an intuitive character is to reason from the end-stage, to judge on the basis of appearance, and to depend on external cues for the determination of good or bad, it is not surprising that he feels many of his problems exist in the circumstances that surround him. Although we sometimes use techniques that help an intuitive internalize his problems, we do not expect to change (see p. 154 and 164) his tendency to view his problems as external. In fact the problems of an intuitive are more often with his social world than with inner conflict. In the intuitive we thus have a paradox: on the one hand, he tends to create problems for himself by seeing all his problems as externally caused. On the other hand, very often these problems he creates for himself are external problems. Efforts are made to help him internalize certain things he sees as external; yet we also try to assist him with some of his external problems. When an intuitive patient tells us that the reason his wife left him is that she found another man, and that he is a victim, we may try to help him identify his role in precipitating her leaving. If some particular behavior on his part resulted in her leaving, he may then choose to give up that particular kind of behavior in an attempt to win her back, or he may decide that his style of behavior is more important to him than continuing the marriage. We may, however, suggest he make efforts to win his wife back and even help him to do so if we think the marriage offers him more stability.

Traditionally, the role of social caseworkers in treating most such patients was to manipulate the environment with the goal of making life better for the patients, while at the same time to help them to adapt to components of the environment that could not be changed. Similarly, we try to help the intuitive to understand and deal with his circumstances. At times we try to "treat" some aspects of his environment. We may interview his spouse or write a letter for him (violations of technique if we planned to analyze the transference). We may work with the patient to help him establish himself within his social support system, his family, school, probation officer, parole officer, work environment. We may gather, or help the patient to gather, information about resources, or refer him to social, health, or legal services. At the very least our approach will be directed toward helping the patient to cope more effectively with social reality.

Project Re-ED (Hobbs, 1975, p. 218–219) was particularly alert to the importance in treatment of the delinquent of a social support system. Re-ED defined the dysfunction of the delinquent as a "manifestation of the breakdown of an ecological system composed of child, family, neighborhood, and community." Re-ED's strategy was "to remove the child, in *space, time,* and *meaning,* the least possible distance from the people with whom he must learn to live, and who, in turn, must learn how to increase their contribution to his full development." The goal was not cure, but "to restore to effective operation the small social system of which the child is an integral part."

Consistency, reliability, and clear definition of boundaries by the therapist are either explicitly or implicitly recommended by those therapists who report some success with behavior disorders. Their approach seems to be to meet the patients where they are—accepting their pursuit of narcissistic supplies and their inability to view attributes in degrees, and helping them to get what they want. We help them to take into account other points of view, not to correct a defect but to help them avoid what might be a source of trouble or to exploit an opportunity.

Synanon, Alcoholics Anonymous, EST, transactional analysis, Project Re-ED, and behavior modification try primarily to change behavior rather than basic intrapsychic orientation. Interaction in the milieu is the primary arena for change in the intuitive. There are some variations in what is stressed in any given approach, e.g., turning action into verbal expression (Greenwald, 1974) or attempting to change the milieu (Hobbs, 1975), but the overall goal is change in expression rather than basic intrapsychic reorganization.

Attempting to turn an intuitive from the pursuit of narcissistic supplies such as material goods and prestige is undesirable not only because it is probably futile but also because such supplies serve to maintain a degree of self-esteem that may be essential to the intuitive's feeling well and even to his stable functioning. Recall Mr. W who (Chapter 5), once depressed, could not sell. Our objective is to teach an intuitive to control his impulses, think or talk instead of acting, and monitor his own social function, all of which should provide a better payoff. We consider it unfeasible to build an internalized, automatic system of conventional–moral values.[18] Improving an intuitive's ability to evaluate consciously sources of potential trouble and the various circumstances offered and to consider these when he acts is for us a suitable treatment objective for such a character type. A goal for the intuitive is en-lightened self-interest; we categorize enlightened self-in-terest as a formal operational correction, a "thinking about thinking," a consideration of the possible outcomes of doing what one feels like doing, a form of hypothetico–deductive social cognition.

Insight for the intuitive is used in the teaching or learning mode.[19] An intuitive character may be taught that his thinking is global and dichotomous, that his social as-sessments are characterized by a black-or-white and all-or-none quality. He may learn through insight of his tenden-cy to believe in immanent justice, to believe that one gets what one deserves and that one deserves what one gets. He may learn about his tendency to externalize, to deny, and to project. To the extent that he develops such self-awareness, he may gain more choice in his behavior and perhaps in his attitudes. If he learns to be alert to his own intuitive-type defenses and mechanisms when they are not beneficial to him, he may be able to make corrections, toward the overall goal of meeting his needs. He may also become less critical of his own needs.

Obviously, the stance of the therapist is not an absti-nent one; rather he is a counselor promising, "I'll show you how to get what you want."[20] With this promise, the thera-pist does his best to help the patient avoid trouble while pursuing narcissistic goals. In taking a nonjudgmental and nonpunitive approach toward pursuing narcissistic sup-plies, the therapist seeks to create a climate in which the patient may feel understood as opposed to humiliated.[21]

The guide counselor, or teacher role we propose im-plies that the therapist knows better than the patient where the patient's welfare best lies. Our rationale for this

attitude is consistent with the formulation that the intuitive patient evaluates what is good for him in terms of
what feels good at the moment. He does not usually integrate what makes him feel good at the moment with what
caused difficulty in the past. (Those intuitives who have
learned to recognize what got them into trouble in the past
do not usually seek treatment.) His system for processing
information does not coordinate the two pieces of information, past and present. Typically he does not postpone
immediate gratification. His experience as a child taught
him that if he did not "get while the getting was good," he
might not get at all. The patient may not be relied upon to
judge what is in his best interest because he has not constructed a reliable system for judging long-term interests.

If the intuitive character experiences the abstinent
stance as a form of feeding, as being taken care of, we
would say that the abstinent stance should not be discontinued nor the patient's experience analyzed. Thus, the
patient's narcissistic wishes are being gratified, but in the
hope of helping him improve his function. Most intuitive
characters will on the contrary experience an abstinent
stance as depriving.

The "Dutch uncle" stance, which includes giving advice, perhaps persuading the patient to try to delay gratification and to consider consequences, is often helpful to
intuitive characters, especially those whose presenting
problem involves getting into trouble because of unacceptable behavior. If such a patient understands the psychotherapeutic experience in the context of someone's being
in his "corner," and the therapist as someone who can
teach him how to meet his needs in ways that do not get
him into trouble, he will improve his current situation and
may learn new coping skills. Of course an intuitive character who is basically distrustful may experience the therapist's attempt to be in his "corner" as the therapist's way
of gaining something for himself. Then the "Dutch uncle"

stance may have to be modified, perhaps by introducing a degree of distance in the relationship or by talking about what the therapist gains.

In this chapter we have suggested overall strategies and major goals for treatment of the intuitive personality. We now wish to make some comments on technique that follow from our conceptualization of the intuitive's needs and style of function, i.e., his seeing things from a single, current, personal perspective. (1) The intuitive needs current gratification, and thus should be praised from time to time. If he delays acting upon impulse in the hopes of a longer-term payoff, one does well to applaud him a little. (2) Interpretation and clarification do not play the same roles as they do in treatment of an operational. Since the intuitive confuses intent with event, the therapist should not be surprised that when inquiries or explanations cause the patient pain, the patient assumes the therapist meant him harm. For that reason, treatment should be sugarcoated, if possible. The therapist may point out the patient's defenses—denial, projection, rationalization—not only as behaviors that may be modified to better meet his needs but also as attributes that are interesting and clever. This positive interest certainly is part of transactional analysis, Synanon, and EST. (3) Genetic insight is not ordinarily helpful to intuitives in our experience, partly because it often causes psychic pain, and may simply depress the patient (see Note 19). However, genetic insight may be used to help an intuitive forgive his caregivers upon recognition that they did as best they could, having had their own problems and typically having experienced deprived or erratic rearing similar to that of the patient.

Similarly although the therapist is alert to recognize with an intuitive his having been treated unfairly by another person, one may take a clinical view of the patient's current or past persecutor. The therapist may ask, "I wonder why he was so rude or so cruel? Was he raised that way? Was he treated that way? Do you know anything about that?" As the patient begins to take a similar view of the persecutor, he may view more kindly the more cruel and selfish aspects of himself, since the persecutor largely functions as repository for projections of the patient's less-desirable characteristics. If the therapist takes too strong a position against a patient's persecutor, it will only strengthen the patient's black-or-white, inside-and-outside system and his need to project.

As separations during therapy are particularly critical in treating intuitives, it is sometimes helpful to assign a task to the patient as is done in behavior modification, making a chart—for example, in regard to dieting or other impulse control—of a current issue in the therapy. The therapist may send the patient a note or bring a gift. The gift should be less a bauble than something that will direct the patient toward longer-term satisfaction, e.g., a book about cats for a cat lover, or a book on wines for an epicure.

Not surprisingly, intuitives understand bargaining, i.e., "If you do this, I'll do that." Sometimes it is best to limit treatment by a very specific contract, e.g., "We will meet for so many sessions to work on such and such." This may limit dependency, hence frustration and humiliation. When bargaining with those intuitives who have difficulty talking because of feelings of humiliation, one may say "It's okay if you turn aside and don't look at me, if you can talk more easily." When the patient asks the therapist about his personal life, the therapist may say, "I'll be glad to answer that, but first tell me why you asked." It is essential that the patient fulfill his part of any bargain first (that you not be manipulable) but also that the therapist carry out his promise (to deliver). Sometimes the therapist is involved in a bargain without knowing it: the patient offers a favor, expecting something in return. It may be wise for the therapist to enter the bargain but to clarify the terms in order to ensure that he is willing to pay the price.

Much of the above—the rewards (applause), the bargaining, the contract, the praise for improved behavior—has earmarks of behavior modification. If there is one character structure more suited than the others for the behavior modification techniques, it surely is the intuitive.

Thus far, all the techniques we have recommended have been part of individual psychotherapy. Group therapy, however, is often a particularly suitable treatment modality for intuitive characters. Group-living experience is intrinsic to a number of programs for the treatment of sociopathic personalities. The external structure helps them to learn new socially adaptive behaviors, just as they learn socially maladaptive behaviors in gangs and prisons. Spread of transference among various institutional workers alleviates some of the burden of treatment. In a group, peers may provide rewards, teaching, protection, and many other functions a guide would serve, which assist the intuitive in modifying behavior and attitudes. Yochelson and Samenow (1976) exploit this approach. An institutional setting may provide ranked groups, with success at one level resulting in graduation to the next level, a narcissistic reward associated with an opportunity to interact in a more advanced group.

With the operational, the stance is one of abstinence, the curative agent is insight, the techniques are interpretation and clarification, and the goal is to make the unconscious conscious in order that the ego be free to make choices. With the intuitive, the stance is one of guiding or teaching, the curative agent is learning and identification, the techniques are suggestion, manipulation, and modeling, and the goals are to avoid trouble and to enhance self-esteem.

Chapter 11

TREATMENT OF THE SYMBOLIC

There is a natural correspondence between obsessive traits and operational character structure and between socio-pathic traits and intuitive character structure. Nevertheless, patients who present as obsessive or sociopathic personalities most often prove to be operational symbolics or intuitive symbolics, i.e., symbolic characters with an operational or intuitive cast. Undermining the personality defenses of an operational symbolic or intuitive symbolic puts at risk a structure that helps deal with the symbolic's identify diffusion. Fortunately some symbolic characters who present with obsessive or sociopathic features are tenacious about holding on to what they have constructed; a therapist who insists on trying to undermine these structures may find himself unemployed. Some symbolic patients tolerate this form of assault, and even benefit—the benefits, we believe, resulting more from the connection with the therapist than from any assault on obsessive or sociopathic traits. Others are too vulnerable to the undermining process: they regress and may even become psychotic.

Whether the object of a symbolic character's complaint is external to himself, as an intuitive symbolic's usually is, or internal, as an operational symbolic's usually is, the boundary between internal and external is blurred for him to some extent. Although his complaint may relate to function or to appearance, any treatment approach designed for a symbolic character best takes into account issues of attachment and identity.

A therapist who works with a symbolic character recognizes that the wish to merge or the fear of merging and the wish to be separate or the fear of separation are major concerns in therapy. We suggest the therapist adopt a stance that conveys his acceptance of these needs without signaling that either total merger or separation is the goal of the therapy. This would seem important for Ms. J (in Chapter 6), who tended to merge, but became dysfunctional when too intimate.

The first step we recommend in the course of treatment with a symbolic is the establishment of a connection. Sometimes if this does not happen in the first interview, the patient discontinues therapy. Typically the symbolic character himself establishes the connection unless the therapist thwarts his attempt by asking too many questions or by failing to acknowledge or to allow the connection.

The goal of a symbolic who seeks treatment is usually to establish or re-establish a sense of wholeness. At some level he hopes by treatment to repair a broken identity or to find one. He is in search of a role, a definition, a purpose, or a place for himself. Thus, generally, we take care not to undermine his defenses, defenses that may even be flimsy and primitive. Uncovering unconscious material may lead to confusion or psychosis, or at least to severe emotional pain. Kohut (1977) suggested that narcissistic personalities, whom we would probably call types of symbolic characters, may benefit from interpretation of their defenses. Generally we think the mechanisms the symbolic character has constructed to deal with his confusion should be respected. We do not aim toward interpretation of defenses or recovery of genetic material or uncovering unconscious motivation. If one undermines narcissistic personality defenses, one risks developing a sick rather than a healthy symbolic.

Many symbolic characters do not have the social cognitive structure to enable integration of fragments. They tend to overconnect, resulting in confusion, further diffusion of ego boundaries, undifferentiation of self and objects (or of part object with whole object, or of part self with whole self) accompanied by intense shifts in affect. We favor helping them to build structure, to separate out bits of identity, to focus on the good parts of themselves, to draw boundaries or to draw distinctions—to intellectualize or isolate or simply not to challenge any such mechanisms that are working.

We do not ordinarily expect a patient to integrate a psychotic experience, but rather to isolate or to repress it, to make it ego-alien. If a patient's system—including repression of a psychotic process—is working well, we probably cannot alter it basically. If it is not working well, we do not take it apart without being sure that it will reassemble with a better balance. Our position is at the opposite end of the spectrum from Volkan's (1976). He takes a position that encourages transference psychosis with the expectation of complete resolution.

An individual who has identity and attachment problems may burden a therapist much more heavily than someone whose problems primarily involve internal conflict or than someone who needs guidance. Even the demands of a well-functioning symbolic character on the therapist may be much greater than that of an operational or intuitive character. The symbolic's demand emanates from his need for a therapist who will share himself. We believe that the essence of psychotherapy with a symbolic character lies in the management of the sharing of connection. Searles (1965), working with schizophrenics, allowed diffusion of his own boundaries, believing that the therapist needs to take the psychotic process into himself. Treatment was complete when the therapist recovered. Our position is less extreme than that of Searles. Nevertheless, when listening, Ms. J's therapist reported feeling ill as he felt the depth of her depression. Ideally the quality of connection or sharing offered is governed by the patient's needs, not the needs of the therapist; sometimes the therapist's limitations may not permit this. Whether or not he can meet the patient's need for sharing, the therapist is best aware of its presence.

Symbolic characters who do not have satisfactory attachments to another person, a social role, a cause, or an activity, feeling that something is missing, seek a sense of wholeness. The subtypes—operational symbolic, intuitive symbolic, mixed, or pure symbolic—may pursue this goal of wholeness through divergent paths. The aims of therapists treating symbolic characters may therefore range widely.

In one instance a therapist may attempt to help a patient who thinks of himself as a bad person to accept the bad qualities of envy, despair, or dependency as part of the human condition and as parts of his particular identity. Some symbolics may be subject to profound internal shifts, depending on changes in their external situation and thus may suffer more than better-defended patients. The therapist may help such a patient to know an identity as a sufferer, or as a very sensitive person; some causes that glorify suffering similarly provide identity for their adherents. In another case or at another phase with the same patient, the therapist may help the patient become aware of and accept his desire to be perfect. The therapist helps the patient to build identity, to define himself (to himself) in terms of his social roles, skills, and allegiances. A therapist may attempt to assist a patient to "hook up" with a relatively stable setting, person, or pursuit. Often a therapist works toward a combination of partial solutions that helps the patient to establish a sense of self and to ward off a sense of emptiness and of lack of direction.

Ms. K complained about overeating and wanted help in trying to stop. She claimed she could not stop because she was "an addict," "a weak person." The therapist, intending to raise her self-esteem, suggested that there was more to her than the attributes of addictiveness and weakness. He pointed to some instances in her past, which she had described to him, in which she had controlled her eating and had been more in charge of herself. By the third interview the patient had become insistent that she really was an addict and a weak person. She would not accept the therapist's efforts to bolster her self-esteem. The therapist thought the patient was trying to engage him in a "power struggle." He felt he could not "reach" her and was concerned that she would discontinue treatment. He failed to recognize that the patient was making an identity statement. She was trying to tell him how she saw herself: she did not see her identity as separate from, or more than, an attribute. She viewed her addiction and weakness, not as a part of her identity, but as her whole self, i.e., a bad person. The therapist by his interventions was showing he would accept her only if she agreed to give up the person she saw herself to be—to stop defining herself in terms of her part. We suggested to the therapist that he accept her as she requested in order to make a connection with her, and that he make interventions calculated to send the message that he understood and accepted her in spite of the fact that she was a defective person. She needed a connection with him, a kind of dual unity in which she could borrow, or identify with, his strength in order to solve her problem. What this patient was asking for reflected her basic investment and her concern about her identity. It also reflected her style of social cognition, i.e., equating the part, her addiction and weakness, with the whole, her identity. Finally, it should be understood that her identity as a defective or weak person was a solution for her, albeit not a satisfactory one.

Identity may rest only on one aspect of a patient's life. Ms. T was brought to treatment by her husband. His company was transferring him to another location; the transfer meant she would have to leave her job. She had been in this area for only a short time, and had left behind her many ties with family and friends in her home community. Her current job provided her with a sense of individual identity. She was frightened that she would merge with her husband and disappear, if she did not have something of her own to hold. She felt disoriented, not in charge of herself, and despairing. For a few days she became mute and sat rocking in a rocking chair that she had inherited from her grandmother. She was about to lose her job, and all she felt she had left of her roots was the rocking chair.

Ms. T's therapist presented himself as open for attachment, and communicated his understanding that her identity was at stake, and that he would like to help and wondered how he might help. He did not attempt to manipulate or coerce her. One of Ms. T's hesitations about seeing a therapist stemmed from her belief that seeing a therapist meant she was crazy. The therapist made no effort to address this belief, but instead worked at "making a connection." Ms. T was very reluctant to come to her appointments. At first she said nothing, and the therapist merely sat with her and talked to her. After several visits she began to talk about the proposed move and her pending job loss. Her crisis passed, and she returned to her job. She and the therapist then started to work on the situation that occasioned her decompensation. She was invested in the belief that anything could be mastered through an act of will, and she needed to view herself as in charge of herself in order to feel whole. What she wanted from treatment was help in regaining the sense of being in charge of herself. The therapist decided not to foster a mergerlike, continuing attachment, knowing that if she did not feel as if she were under her own auspices she would become psychotic. He explained the crisis to her as resulting from her tendency to inhibit her expression of feelings. (The therapist learned that the patient wanted to go along with her husband's transfer and that she believed one should be able to master all problems oneself. Consequently she did not tell her husband of her problems, but rather became confused and fell mute.) In the process of acknowledging this she also began to look at her inclination to try to control the future instead of "taking one step at a time," "each day as it comes along." She brought up practical problems with the therapist, and asked and heeded his advice. She generalized, distilling from the advice principles, that she applied to other situations, making her both less dependent on the therapist for specific advice and less attached to him. An example was the time she asked the therapist how he thought she should explain to her colleagues her absence from work. He suggested that she did not have to answer to her colleagues, that as a person she was entitled to have problems and to do whatever she had to in order to cope. After this, she permitted herself to express her feelings to her husband on the grounds that she was entitled to do what she needed to do in order to cope with her problems. Before moving to the new location Ms. T secured a job there, establishing both a connection and a "piece" of identity.

We tend to draw from the literature on the treatment of the narcissistic and borderline personalities when discussing treatment of the symbolic character. This does not mean we think that most symbolics are borderline or narcissistic personalities.[22] Rather we think that although the literature deals with "sick" symbolics, it also addresses certain basic factors that all symbolics share.

We and other therapists like ourselves, accept the patient's basic structure and work toward relief of pain and improvement of function with a reasonable degree of stability. That is, we work toward growth within the parameters of symbolic character structure. Other therapists try to change the character structure of borderline and narcissistic patients.

Masterson (1976) endeavored to break the investment in attachment of borderlines so that they could be centered in themselves and function as separate and individuated. His goal of getting the patient to abandon clinging behavior, thus rekindling "the individuation process," may be achievable in some of the patients he treats.[23] Although their overt clinging behavior disappears, we suspect his patients retain their investment in attachment and continue to use preconceptual reasoning, thus still defining themselves in terms of parts and externals.[24]

A 45-year-old man returned to Masterson (1976) for treatment for a third time. As the patient became more committed to the therapy than to his clinging behavior outside therapy, he began to be more self-expressive and more self-assertive, which Masterson regarded as signs of individuation. Eventually the patient saw his mother, his father, and himself as separate and whole objects, each having both good and bad qualities. At this point the patient was motivated by his own thoughts and feelings—differentiated—in Masterson's view.

Masterson expressed a lingering doubt about this patient being ready to terminate therapy because the patient was handling his feelings of separation from the therapist by acting them out rather than by working through them. At the patient's insistence, therapy was discontinued. Concerned that individuation was incomplete Masterson invited the patient to return at a later date. We wonder if this final move on Masterson's part served to maintain the patient's attachment to him. If that is so, it constitutes good treatment, but the patient has not given up attachment. The patient discontinued shortly after Masterson returned from a month's vacation. A few months previously, when the patient was talking about Masterson's not giving him love or acceptance, Masterson told the patient that he was angry because Masterson would not parent him. The patient told Masterson that Masterson was like his father who expected him to grow up in order to earn his love. The patient also suggested decreasing the frequency of interviews and talked about dreams and fantasies of unconditional love. Following this he told about his parents' being phony and their trying to impose their values on him in order to make him feel bad. In this context he became more insistent that he was going to decrease the frequency of his sessions. When Masterson interpreted this as resistance, the patient said that Masterson was like his parents who wanted him to do things their way; he said he wanted to do this (reduce the frequency of sessions) his own way. Masterson again interpreted the resistance, saying that reducing the frequency of sessions was a way of avoiding individuation. The themes in the patient's last few sessions were that he feared separation from Masterson, that he could not individuate and didn't want to, and that individuation meant death. As this patient left before individuation appeared complete and was invited to return, he may not have had to give up either his connection to Masterson or his general investment in attachment.

Masterson's (1976) value system was part of his goal for the patient. He believed that "with a separate and defined self-image, an autonomous and reality oriented ego, and a whole object relations unit, the patient's individuation flowers and new capacities emerge for love and work that are the true building blocks for gratification in adult life" (p. 94). He contrasted the American form of childraising with that of the kibbutz, whose children, according to certain studies, made excellent soldiers, scholars, and citizens, but lacked capacities for intimacy, autonomy, and creativity. Masterson (1985, p. 95) wrote that "intimacy, autonomy and creativity . . . are the essence of what makes us human."

Our idea of satisfactory treatment for the symbolic character differs greatly from Masterson's treatment of the borderline disorders. A symbolic character may be thought of as cured when he has developed a system for continuing a partly externalized, partly internalized connection with the therapist. One way a symbolic character may maintain such a connection is by imitating some aspect of the therapist: copying the therapist's way of speaking or dressing, smoking a cigar or growing a beard, perhaps pursuing the same profession as the therapist. (When an identification is made, there is perhaps less need for ongoing connection to the therapist.) Some symbolic patients maintain their connection after formal termination by sending their therapist a Christmas report card that outlines their problems and progress for that year. Others return for a "shot in the arm" or "refresher" visit from time to time or make an occasional telephone call to the therapist. Metaphorically speaking, the connection between the symbolic patient and the therapist is like a cord that is not cut, though it may become loose and longer and thinner. While Masterson (1976) views this ongoing contact as incomplete treatment and as belonging to the supportive phase of treatment, Bowlby (1985), Kohut (1977), Zetzel (1971), and we tend to think of it as part of successfully completed treatment. Many symbolic characters fully terminate the connection with the therapist. We think these individuals transfer their attachment to another person or to some activity or cause.

Our position is that for the treatment of borderline and narcissistic patients, who generally have symbolic character structures, the therapist should be available for the degree of attachment that is comfortable and functional for the patient. The therapist must protect certain patients, for example Ms. T or Ms. J, by limiting the degree of attachment if it threatens to cause pain, dysfunction, or a loss of identity. The therapist respects the patient's need for attachment or for avoidance of attachment, the coping mechanisms the patient has established, and any identity or pieces of identity the patient has constructed.

We agree with Zetzel's (1971) belief that the therapist should present himself to the patient a real person and offer the patient a real relationship. It should be understood that this does not mean a personal relationship, although the therapist may accept the patient's need to think of the therapist as part of himself. As the therapist may participate in a dual unity, a kind of symbiotic relationship with the patient, the therapist also seeks to convey at times that he is a human being with needs of his own. Unlike Kernberg (1975), we suggest that early in the treatment a therapist may indicate certain individual preferences or eccentricities, not so much to provide a model for identification but to help define himself for the patient. This does not give the therapist license to reveal himself for his own gratification or to reveal himself in such detail as to burden or disillusion the patient. To some extent the therapist also lets the patient know what he can provide and what he can put up with from the patient. The dual unity is limited. The therapist is "responsive," in Kohut's (1977) meaning, to the patient. He attempts to convey that he understands the patient and can feel what the patient is feeling. In order to do this he responds, as Kohut tells us, from a deep level within himself. The therapist tries not to convey that he and the patient are one person, but rather that they are two parts of the dual unity. There is a boundary to the therapist which the patient will encounter from time to time during the course of their relationship. This boundary lets the patient know that the therapist is a real person and not a part of the patient. The boundary also may be necessary to protect the therapist. The therapist, in fairness to himself and the patient, must know the limits of burden he is willing to carry as attachment develops.

The therapist who works with a symbolic character must make a decision as to whether or not he will honor the patient's wish for or fear of merger with him. In managing attachment the therapist decides, on the basis of his overall goal for a particular patient in treatment, whether it would be beneficial or detrimental to the patient to allow him to attach to the therapist. We discourage attachment or merger whenever it will make the patient paranoid, cause him to feel fragmented or confused, or perhaps scare him into leaving therapy.

The patient will likely test whether the therapist will allow him to attach or avoid attachment, i.e., whether the therapist will allow him to make the kind of connection he needs in order to work in therapy. Paranoid and schizoid personalities, who are afraid of merging, still need to make a connection with the therapist. But it is a limited connection in that the patient sets certain boundaries and the therapist abides by them. For example, early in treatment a patient with a paranoid personality may let it be known that he will not tolerate intrusive questioning. The therapist who expects to make a connection with such a patient honors that limit.

Sometimes a patient, because of his fear of fragmentation or depression, is so desperate for attachment that he clings to a relationship or situation, e.g., a marriage or a job, no matter how unsatisfactory. The more dependent the patient becomes on this external source for self-definition and valuation, the more powerful the person or situation becomes to him, and the more inclined he is to project his own feelings onto that person or situation. For example, feelings of anger, suppressed in order to retain the object, may be projected upon a spouse who the patient feels is abusive (see Ms. J). A therapist should be alert to the prospect that a similar circumstance may arise in the therapeutic relationship unless he is careful to define the boundary between himself and the patient.

One such patient told his therapist that he did not want to speak about a particular aspect of his life because he was afraid that, if he got started, he would "spill his guts." This could have been interpreted by the therapist as lack of trust. Instead the therapist, understanding the tenuous nature of the patient's identity and his need to attach to others for self-definition and self-worth, told the patient that although it was usually good to talk about everything in psychotherapy, it was also good that the patient could decide what he wished to share with the therapist and what he wanted to keep to himself. In this way the therapist attempted to educate the patient to the idea that he and the therapist were two separate people and that there were things that belonged to the patient and not to the therapist. The patient was entitled to choose whether or not he wished to share a particular piece of his own business with the therapist. (The therapist who treated Ms. T was similarly careful to allow her to choose what to discuss.)

Making a connection and communicating to the patient that the therapist understands and wants to help are not accomplished in the same way with all symbolic characters. Some symbolics, like Mr. B (in Chapter 8), may interpret a therapist's silence as understanding and connectedness. It is necessary for the therapist to know how the patient is experiencing the psychotherapeutic situation in order to decide whether or not to keep quiet.

Treatment typically begins with the patient forming a kind of symbiotic tie to the good mother. At some point the therapist will do something that breaks the connection, e.g., withdrawing support or attention or saying "no" to the patient. With the break in the tie, the patient becomes disillusioned, sometimes depressed, hostile, envious. He feels deserted and may manifest hatred and fear of the therapist. Because the symbolic character typically does not distinguish the identity of a person from the attributes of that person, he interprets his therapist's unempathic behavior as meaning that the therapist is a bad or an incompetent person. The patient then feels the therapist should be controlled, defeated, denounced, ridiculed, all of which the patient may or may not tell the therapist [but all about which Kohut (1977), warned us]. If the wish for the symbiotic bond is very strong, the patient will try to suppress negative feelings or to apologize for any that slip out. The therapist's task is to recognize when the connection has been broken, and unexpressed negative feelings are present. How he will handle the situation will depend upon his treatment goal for that particular patient.

Sometimes when the tie has been broken the therapist may tell the patient that he, the therapist, feels he has done something to estrange the patient and would like the patient's aid in examining what has happened. If the therapist is not attuned to the breaking of the tie and if he does not somehow reestablish it, succeeding sessions will be empty and the patient will eventually drop out of treatment. The therapist who has had experience with these patients often knows exactly when the connection breaks. If it is early in treatment, he may elect to mend it quickly without any verbal acknowledgment. He may make a gesture that indicates he is back together with the patient again. With a patient whom the therapist has reason to believe is capable of constructing a partially separate identity, the therapist may choose to let the estrangement continue until the patient decides to verbalize his feelings. This is somewhat dangerous because the therapist assumes the patient will disclose his negative feelings rather than discontinue treatment. In a case in which the estrangement is allowed to continue, when the patient reveals his feelings, the therapist may suggest, "I have disappointed you, and now you see me as a bad person." Generally speaking, the therapist accepts and even solicits the expression of negative feelings toward himself. Furthermore, as Hill (1955) recommended, the therapist should usually admit a mistake, for example, a lapse of attention, but should insist that his general intention is therapeutic. He may elect to point out the patient's tendency to split, i.e., to see the therapist as an omniscient, benevolent person at times and as an evil person at other times. By such actions the therapist hopes that the patient will come to view the therapist in some measure as neither a "saint" nor a "devil" but as a real person with good and bad attributes. In our opinion, although treatment cannot "heal" this split or eliminate splitting as a mechanism, learning that he has such a tendency may help the patient. The patient may eventually learn to remind himself when he sees only one side of an issue, that a another side exists. This reminder is a formal operational correction: it is thinking about thinking. We will review this again in Chapter 13.

With symbolic characters who are schizophrenic,[25] a severe communication problem may arise as they speak metaphorically or in sentence fragments. At such times the therapist may not understand what the patient is trying to communicate. The therapist must send the message through words and demeanor that he is truly interested in understanding and communicating with the person. The widely divergent approaches of Rosen and Schwing had this in common (Stone, 1984). The importance of establishing contact with a schizophrenic was also later emphasized by Huszonek (1987). For the schizophrenic patient the therapist's understanding him, i.e., establishing communication, sometimes constitutes the treatment. The feeling of being understood provides at once both connection and definition and the ultimate support.

The therapist's feeling of being cut off by faulty communication with the patient may reflect the patient's feeling of being cut off from the therapist. This is a cue to examine what has broken the connection. The break may be a response to perceived slights by the therapist such as tardiness, interruptions during the therapy session, or apparent preoccupation or overenthusiasm. The patient may view any of these as negative communications from the therapist. No tacit understanding should go unchallenged (Hill, 1955). For example, one should not assume that a brief telephone interruption is of no consequence. When the therapist experiences a communication cutoff, rather than trying to examine together with the patient what has occurred, he may elect to examine his own psyche to understand a break in "empathic immersion" [Kohut's term, (1977)]. Usually the patient will allow the offending therapist a chance to repair the break.

When the therapist, from his experience with a particular patient, knows that the connection is again being tested or needs reinforcing, mirroring the patient's feelings may be useful. A facial expression, gesture, or interested posture may suffice. When the patient is describing some future event, which the therapist knows is frightening to the patient, the therapist may show consternation or may exclaim, "Oh, no!" This can be relieving to the patient who then experiences the therapist as sharing his feelings. The therapist's tone and expression should convey that although the event is scary, it is lifesize and, therefore, manageable and tolerable.

With one patient a therapist often used the word "we," and thus identified himself with some aspect of the patient. Because this patient was in a profession similar to the therapist's, they sometimes discussed professional problems together. The therapist's use of "we" emphasized their similar problems and reinforced the tie between them. This patient was successful professionally, had established a stable schizoid lifestyle, and continued to see the therapist regularly, if infrequently.

A therapist who works with symbolic characters must accept his own fallibility. Although a patient may try to engage the therapist's feeling that he is omnipotent or omniscient, the therapist should not feel he must be either of these for the patient. [Nevertheless, like Kohut (1977), a therapist may allow this idealizing to take place and to go unanalyzed, in certain symbolics.] This contrasts with the treatment of the operational, in which the patient is allowed initially to see the therapist as omnipotent but whose transference is later analyzed. Still differently, the intuitive is helped to experience the therapist as powerful and able to lead the way. A symbolic character may have trouble accepting himself as human, feeling he is either perfect or unacceptable. He may believe he must change any qualities that he perceives as negative in himself. A therapist who is unaccepting of his own faults, and therefore is likely judgmental of others, may reinforce the need for perfection in such a symbolic character. Identification with a self-accepting human being—the therapist—may help the patient accept his negative qualities as part of human nature and as pieces of his identity. With such a symbolic it may be important from the outset that the patient acknowledge the therapist's limitations.

Many symbolic characters as children have experienced role reversal in their relationship with the mothering person, and thus may take a mothering or caregiving role. The therapist's acceptance of help from the patient may help the patient feel more in control and so feel more like himself. The patient defines the relationship and has a nonthreatening tie with the therapist.

The therapist should be alert to the fact that role reversal may occur even when he is not attempting to use it. When the patient brings "goodies," it may be obvious. Role reversal, however, may be expressed by a patient's talking about a subject he has reason to believe is interesting or beneficial to the therapist. The patient may be entertaining the therapist or taking care of the therapist's needs in order to strengthen the tie between them or to insure that the therapist owes him care in return. Some symbolic characters will pay any price for attachment. The therapist must consider whether the patient's caregiving in this instance is a benefit or a detriment to the patient. It may or may not be helpful to analyze these gifts.

The patient's smallest achievements sometimes merit the therapist's recognition and safeguarding. Because the patient reasons from part to part, he may in large measure define and value himself with each step he takes. If he has a success, he is a successful person; conversely, if he has a failure, he is a "zero." Each bit of progress may bolster his confidence, his sense of self, and his ability to take the next step.

We usually support rather than interpret defenses of a symbolic character. Insight into defenses and other aspects of the symbolic may, however, may be turned to support and define him, if the therapist presents the understanding as something of special interest or as a bit of identity that the patient may use to define himself. At times it is appropriate to help a symbolic character invoke certain defenses, such as externalization and intellectualization, defenses that enable him to take distance. With one patient who reported an experience in which one could infer that she was angry it was not helpful to ask her if it had made her mad. The patient felt she should be above feeling anger. She suffered from depression and used alcohol as her comforter. What seemed to work was the therapist's saying, "Oh, no. That makes me so mad," or "He shouldn't have done that." These interventions placed the judgment and focus outside the patient. She was able to project out and separate herself from the bad object. Not only was the patient's self-esteem enhanced and her depression eased but also her self- and object representations had greater stability. Such externalization helped her construct an identity.

When a patient has begun to fragment or disorganize, telling the patient something about himself is particularly useful in helping him to reorganize. Statements such as "You're an in-charge person" or "You are a very sensitive person" may be a nucleus around which the patient reconstructs a sense of who he is. For Ms. D (Chapter 8), for example, being "vulnerable to stress" was an element of identity.

Frequently a symbolic character, learning of his tendency to cling to others, to define himself by his social role, to assume a caregiving stance, or to use a particular defense, will ask "How do I get rid of it?" Cognizant of the importance of preserving the patient's identity, the therapist assures the patient that this tendency is a part of who the patient is, not something to be "gotten rid of" but rather something to be recognized and befriended. Recognition and acceptance of his parts, i.e., his attributes, are essential to the symbolic patient's comfort and good functioning; we believe "exorcising" pieces of identity is counterproductive.

If the therapist directs the treatment toward building instead of undermining structure, he needs to know the strengths as well as the vulnerabilities of the structure. He is interested in the range of the patient's coping skills, the strength of his defensive structure, and the nature of his motives or investment (in addition to his major investment in attachment). The therapist respects any part identity his patient has constructed, even though it may be the identity of a bad person or a weak person.

Clues to what specific identity type will suit a particular patient may be evident from the patient's previous solutions, e.g., the choice of a hippie or a punk-rocker lifestyle. We are inclined to emphasize the less prestigious solution, because old solutions, although at times counterculture, were chosen by the patient because of their particular suitability for him. We could as readily have men-

tioned being a college professor or vice-president of a
bank, but we wish to stress that less culturally sanctioned
identity solutions may have value.

A very intelligent intuitive symbolic's closest childhood friends became criminals, one of whom wound up
on death row. Our patient, in small steps—each step a bit
ahead of disaster, as the authorities (e.g., the judge, his
captain in the Army) were about to close in on him—was
able to take a more conforming tack, until he finished
school as an accountant. As an accountant, his function
became to audit middle and upper management and to
report directly to the board of directors of the corporation.
His identity as a "stoolie" served intuitive and symbolic
functions and represented both a normal and socially desirable (and lucrative) solution, which was not challenged
in the therapy.

In treatment of the symbolic we offer ourselves for
attachment; in treatment of the intuitive we try to be a
guide. In both cases we obscure the pure abstinent atmosphere that fosters and highlights transference and makes
it available for interpretation. If there is a transference interpretation to be made in treating the intuitive it is of his
misunderstanding of our effort to be a guide. If there is a
transference interpretation to be made in treating the symbolic, it is of his failure to recognize our trying to "be in it
with him" or our trying to point the way or of his failure to
accept our limitations in such efforts.

Thus far our focus has been the symbolic aspects of
symbolic characters. What about the fact that many of our
symbolics are operational symbolics or intuitive symbolics? How do we approach their operational or intuitive
qualities? Before we address this we remind ourselves that
our treatment approach must take into account their attachment and identity issues and their preconceptual social cognition. Whether the symbolic character is an operational symbolic, an intuitive symbolic, or a pure or mixed

symbolic, he is basically invested in issues of identity and attachment and brings these investments to psychotherapy. When the therapist focuses treatment around other issues and ignores the issues of primary investments, the symbolic character regardless of subtype often feels that he is not understood. Communicating to the symbolic character that he is understood is critical in treating him. Nevertheless a patient who is a symbolic character of either the intuitive or operational subtype will have issues associated with these other character structures, along with issues associated with the basic symbolic character structure.

Operational symbolics whose attachment and identity issues have been settled, at least for the time being, by their having made a satisfactory connection to someone or something may be experiencing conflict or discomfort about issues having to do with function. In our opinion, a dual approach is indicated for such patients. By this we mean that the therapist may offer interpretations similar to those offered to an operational character and may to a degree take a stance appropriate for an operational. But the stance taken should not be as stringent as one taken with a pure operational character; the stance the therapist takes should be experienced by the patient as one of connection with the therapist. Although the stance appropriate for an operational is useful for this patient, we suspect that real healing is accomplished through the connection and identity definition offered. Certainly creating a context that fails to serve the needs of the symbolic may cause him unnecessary pain or even damage or encourage him to leave treatment.

In our judgment, most of the cases in the psychotherapeutic and psychoanalytic literature have been drawn from a continuum of what we call operational symbolic characters. [Freud's (1959a) case history of the Rat Man (1909) is one of the few detailed presentations of the analysis of a patient we would call a pure operational character.] Perhaps one reason for the large body of literature on "the psychoanalytic situation" is that many of the patients who are in analysis have a symbolic character structure, whether they are ill or well. Freud's (1959b) original description of the recommended psychoanalytic relationship applied to treatment of the good analysand, who we call an operational character and who is not the usual patient. We also think that certain psychoanalysts modify traditional psychoanalysis because they understand the dynamics of these patients whom we call symbolics. We read analysts' accounts of patients, whom they diagnosed with one or another type of neurotic disorder, who qualify for our definition of symbolic character, and whom the analysts treat in the way we recommend for treating symbolic characters. They call the treatment psychoanalysis and credit insight as the curative agent. We think otherwise.

Some patients with symbolic character structure, whom we call mixed symbolics, have a mixture of operational and intuitive characteristics. Depending on the weight of these characteristics, i.e., whether the person is more operational or more intuitive, the therapeutic stance taken is more like analysis or more like guidance, respectively.

Kernberg (1975) proposed that some patients with borderline personality organization may be successfully analyzed whereas others are treatable only by a supportive approach. He recommended a modified form of psychoanalysis for most patients with borderline personality organization; he stated that "the goal of ego strengthening is ever present in this expressive, psychoanalytically oriented treatment" (p. 105). Because he defined the primitive defensive system of the borderline personality organization as pathological and ego weakening, a major objective of treatment was to "undo" (work through) these defenses in order to replace them with repression and other higher-level defenses, thus strengthening the ego. Although partial conflict resolution results from this psychoanalytically oriented treatment approach, Kernberg viewed ego strengthening, not conflict resolution, as the major goal of treatment with these patients.

Masterson (1976) understood identity diffusion to be the essence of borderline pathology, whereas Kernberg (1975) conceived of identity diffusion as but one of the characteristics of a lower level of ego organization. For both authors, autonomy, or the ability of the patient to "cut off" or break the connection with the therapist and to function as a separate individual, was the desired outcome of treatment. Although he acknowledge it might "help the patient to achieve more adaptive patterns of living," Kernberg felt supportive therapy might contribute to an "interminable psychotherapeutic relationship."

Kohut's (1977) treatment goal for patients with narcissistic disorders, whom we see as symbolic, was to help them to build a more cohesive self, filling in the primary defect of the self or rehabilitating its compensatory structures. Cure has taken place and termination is deemed appropriate either when the primary defect of the self is exposed and filled in by working through and transmuting internalizations so that the formerly defective structures are now functioning reliably, or when the patient has achieved mastery of the defenses surrounding the primary defect of the self and these compensatory defensive structures are functioning reliably. Complete filling of the primary defect is not necessary as long as the compensatory structures have been rehabilitated. Separation–individuation or autonomous identity is thus not the ultimate goal of Kohut's treatment approach.

Other psychoanalysts (Bowlby, 1969; Zetzel, 1971) did not think it essential that the patient be "finished" at the end of therapy. Bowlby remained indefinitely available to the patient after the initial formal treatment was over. Zetzel saw treatment as directed toward "developmental

Table 2. Treatment Classification

Character type	Stance	Therapeutic agent	Technique	Goal
Operational	Abstinent	Insight, including working through Identification	Interpretation Clarification	Make the unconscious conscious Ego to be free to choose Increase sense of mastery
Intuitive	Guidance	Learning Identification	Modeling Advising Bargaining Teaching Positive reinforcement Helping to internalize or intellectualize	Maximize gratification while avoiding trouble Increase self-esteem and self-acceptance
Symbolic	Offering appropriate degree of attachment	Attachment Identification Learning	Managing attachment Helping separate self from nonself Modeling Mirroring Positive reinforcement Strengthening self-definition and defenses Helping to externalize	Develop sense of identity or wholeness, not emptiness Increase of self-esteem and self-acceptance Increase in defenses

progress." Her goal was consistent with her understanding of borderline pathology as a developmental failure to achieve (1) definitive self-object differentiation; (2) the capacity to recognize, tolerate, and master separation/loss and narcissistic injury; and most important, (3) the internalization of an ego identification and self-esteem that permits genuine autonomy and maintenance of stable one-to-one relationships. Zetzel believed that the borderline patient's limited capacity to internalize sufficiently stable ego identifications enabling one to become genuinely autonomous accounted for many such patients remaining in treatment interminably. Although borderline patients may not be able to tolerate the painful affect involved in insight-oriented treatment, in Zetzel's experience many proved capable of maintaining a high degree of adaptation if the therapist remained potentially available to them over an indefinite period.

Our goals in treatment of any patient are for him to feel better, for his to function better, and for these improvements to have some stability. In a symbolic, the improvements may involve his constructing more effective coping and defensive skills [much like Kohut's (1977) goal of reparative defensive structure]; developing some self-awareness and self-acceptance; and understanding his basic needs, investment, and way of processing social and emotional information. These accomplishments, although significant, are not "from-the-ground-up" restructuring, with replacement of the old foundation by a new one; they are more a "patching" of the old foundation and perhaps some "upper-story remodeling." On theoretical and clinical grounds, as mentioned previously, we believe character structure, once set, does not change.

See Table 2 for a summary of treatment, considerations as a function of our three types of character structure.

Chapter 12

ADDITIONAL CONSIDERATIONS IN DESIGN OF A TREATMENT PLAN

In the last four chapters we focused primarily on the therapeutic relationship, i.e., the context and stance, which to us is the most important factor in psychotherapy. We believe character structure implies the appropriate context for therapy, hence the corresponding stance to be taken by the therapist. Nevertheless the psychotherapeutic relationship is not the only factor in designing a treatment plan for a particular patient. When we recommend a particular stance because of a person's character structure, we address who that person is at a fundamental level. Yet we must take into account his other attributes and what is going on with him currently, if we are to develop a specific plan for him as an individual. Of course these other attributes, including what is going on with him are not entirely separate from his character structure. Sometimes we may construct a highly specific plan for a patient as we did for Ms. N (in Chapter 2). Often, however, our plan is only a general one, embracing what is likely to work for the patient. We are then ready to support such possibilities when the patient considers or begins a new enterprise. For example, we could not have predicted that Mr. C (in

Chapter 2) would become a computer repairman, but were not surprised when he did and could understood that this occupation suited him, because we knew he liked to work independently and with his hands.

Patients usually point toward solutions. Ms. J (in Chapter 6) became dysfunctional when she was too close to others, was more in control when able to maintain distance, yet felt lost when alone. If Ms. J found a job that involved travel between specific home bases or if she decided to have multiple lovers, we might decide to support such choices, solutions that provide distance but maintain connections. We might also help her to exploit her intuitive tendencies.

Personality organization—usually integral to a patient's psychic economy—may function as a solution to what otherwise could be a chaotic intrapsychic situation. For example, schizoid mechanisms, such as geographic and psychological distancing, may make a patient less vulnerable to merger. In formulating a treatment plan we would want to consider whether we should interfere with such solutions.

We formulate a plan early in treatment, realizing that any treatment plan is subject to revision. We do not think that there is only one treatment plan for a patient and that the therapist must discover that plan. We think the patient may be treated successfully by different means, just as depression may be resolved through medication, shifting of goals, or by overcoming an obstacle to the original goal (Malerstein, 1968). If a symptom or a clinical syndrome is the final common pathway for a complex of organic and psychological factors, as it is beginning to appear is the case in panic attacks, obsessive–compulsive symptoms, manic–depressive psychosis, and schizophrenia, then psychotherapy, environmental manipulation, and drug treatment may each, when appropriate, effect a favorable solution, a favorable final common pathway.

Most patients who have not been forced into treatment move toward restoration of their premorbid balance or toward a better balance. They will assimilate the treatment provided, to the extent they can, to achieve a condition that is less painful and works better. The same thing may not necessarily be said about a natural inclination toward long-term stability (see the discussion of Ms. S in Chapter 4). When we emphasize what the patient makes of the treatment regardless of the therapist, we do not imply that for the therapist "anything goes" and that the patient's drive toward health will take care of everything. Nonetheless even in a classic, well-conducted psychoanalysis—probably the most ordered, systematized therapy to date—obviously different content and organizations are perceived and analyzed differently by analysts. The content and the order of topics or themes must vary markedly depending upon who the analyst is and upon the analysand's state and stage, as well as his outside life.

When formulating a treatment plan it is sometimes useful to pose certain questions. What does the patient say he wants, what does he really want, what does he need? Certain patients, particularly intuitive characters, ask for treatment for depression, for example, when they want to get out of a difficult situation and intend to use being in treatment as an alibi. Other patients may present symptoms as "a ticket of admission," feeling that their real source of concern may not merit a therapist's attention. Some patients may not complain of any symptoms, yet the signs of depression or anxiety are evident and merit attention. Ms. L (Chapter 5) was already working on trying to understand what caused her homicidal thoughts. Although Mr. W (in Chapter 5) began to speak as if he were interested in working on some of his own inner defects, he used most of his hour to focus on what was wrong with the external world. He was not clear or at least not open about what he wanted. Ms. J claimed she wanted to work on some problems, but wanted to merge and be taken care of. We knew closeness and dependency worsened her condition. She would have liked to turn over her global, undifferentiated problems to the therapist, but both she and therapist had to be protected from such an attempt.

Sometimes a patient wants permission to do something or wants to be told what to do. One man wanted to be told to value his career first and not to marry the woman he was dating: he was fearful of merging with her. He told of a previous contact with a psychotherapist who helped him in similar circumstances. We knew our supporting his wish would be helpful to him. We considered, however, whether he might be capable of dealing with (and feel better for handling) both his career and a close personal relationship, although usually the patient's judgment is correct in such matters.

Ms. S was relatively satisfied when she left treatment, having dismissed her lover as unworthy. Nonetheless, since she seemed to have acquired no new techniques in the course of therapy, her improvement was most likely very unstable. If we could have helped her to develop some capacity for enlightened self-interest, she might have then protected herself somewhat as opportunities occurred.

When the presenting complaint is offered by someone other than the patient, such as a spouse or a boss, it is often expressed in terms of that second person's discomfort with the patient's pain or dysfunction. The expectation is usually that the problem will disappear.

If the patient himself initiates treatment we also question why the patient is asking for treatment at this time. What has shifted? Is there something we may do to restore the working balance? Some patients, usually intuitives or intuitive symbolics, whose focus is the "here and now," may come to treatment following a breakup with a lover. All they may want or need is to keep "afloat" by holding on to the therapist until a new lover comes along. Symbolic characters, whose identity is dependent on externals such as social role, another person, or a cause, sometimes come for help when this "connection" has broken. Although a therapist may consider what can be done to help the patient become more adaptable to threatened or actual losses in the future, he must also consider whether certain external agents should be mustered to restore or replace the connection.

If the patient is financially able, has enough time, and presents with an intrapsychic conflict that he would like to better understand, a therapist probably does not have to thoroughly assess the patient's social situation. However, a number of patients seek psychotherapy when the intrapsychic problem is complicated by external circumstances.

Even a good analysand, with time and money, may not want or need a "complete" analysis. Inducing such a patient to continue therapy may be countertherapeutic in a basic sense that then makes any other gains problematic, because the transference in regard to who owns his function may be confounded.

We do not see cultural factors as separate from character structure. Thus we do not think such factors require special consideration in designing a treatment plan, except that the culture of the patient may inform the therapist about the patient and his character structure. As mentioned before, we disagree with therapists whose treatment plan for patients who come from extended family systems includes insight into their interdependent systems with the intent of making the patient less dependent. We think such therapists undermine these patients' adaptive systems in the name of insight and autonomy.

In an extended family system, which is characteristic of many, if not most, cultures in the world, interdependence and traditional roles are valued, and it is expected that a child construct a role identity rather than an identity as a separate individual. If in addition the culture is highly authoritarian and emphasizes "shaming," the child will probably construct a heteronomous rather than autonomous social-ego. Such a person, as an adult, will probably best function in prescribed roles in a system that tells him what is good and bad, rather than in a system that expects him to make such judgments using an internalized system of values for which he must coordinate different perspectives and establish hierarchies of values.

We are particularly interested in any past solutions, especially for the symbolic. What has worked for the patient in the past? What has characterized the roles, settings, and relationships? Characteristics of these previous interactions will probably be reflected in any successful treatment plan. As important as the content of a patient's complaint is its structure, i.e., whether the complaint is external or internal, global or specific, or one of appearance or of function. It is expected that the structural style will be part of a successful outcome.

Finally, we ask what the therapist is willing and able to do. The therapist's personal limitations and his countertransference to a particular patient must be taken into consideration in designing a treatment plan. Searles (1965) allowed a psychotic-like merger to occur with certain patients. However, not every therapist is sufficiently comfortable allowing such intensity. Some therapists feel an aversion to such "draining" patients, and take a management approach to them, often with satisfactory results. Other therapists find action-oriented patients irritating, but because limit setting is often an appropriate technique for such patients, a therapist who feels irritated with continual acting out can often set better limits than one who is not annoyed by action and is therefore too permissive. Still other therapists find those patients who undo and intellectualize boring. Certain patients may need to be referred to someone else. It is unlikely that we are each good with all types of patients.

Part IV

THEORETICAL CONSIDERATIONS

Chapter 13

INSIGHT, LEARNING, AND MERGER

Psychological change is not confined to the treatment room. A friend, a lover, an adversary, or a group, by intended or unintended interaction, may have a lasting psychological effect. Even a physical experience—flying in an airplane, being caught in a fire, exposure to persistent weather, the monsoons, or long winters—may induce one to modify psychologically. A person is a psychobiological organism in an ecological, predominantly sociocultural, system. Modification of any part of the system may affect the person favorably or unfavorably, in whole or in part.

In most instances the individual moves toward adaptation, assimilating what is useful from experience, and either holds his ground or learns from his experience. Thus most of the time he remains relatively stable or improves. Sometimes, however, either because the person makes self-destructive adaptations or because an experience undoes a particular part of him or overwhelms him, he experiences difficulty that requires professional help.

Although psychotherapy has no patent in the psychological arena, it may be powerful. The distinctions we professionals may claim are that our intent is therapeutic and that we have had both training and experience at helping persons who have psychological problems. Of special importance in psychotherapy is our conceptualization of how people tick and how the particular patient we are treating appears to tick; our therapeutic intent requires us, however, to alter our concepts and consequently our interventions based on the patient's response to our interventions and based to some extent on what is happening in the patient's life outside of therapy. What is therapeutic in psychotherapy depends on the patient's use of the therapist's interventions. In turn, how the patient uses an intervention varies considerably depending on his character structure.

INSIGHT

Insight as a means of cure has recently fallen from favor, but for some patients insight, the "Aha" experience, is therapeutic. In such instances the patient realizes or puts together something that he never realized or put together before. This realization may change his perspective on a central problem or issue. Psychoanalysis, in pure form, is confined to interpretation and clarification and directed toward insight into the unconscious motives and defenses that determine behavior. Although a particular insight may be lost and need to be worked through, it is expected that the analysand be treated primarily by insight.[26] Recall the two operational characters, Ms. A (Chapter 9), who thought the therapist had sent her a brochure for an accounting course, and Mr. M (Chapter 11), who expected not to be accountable for a missed appointment because it was outside his control. Both used the therapist's interpretation to gain insight, including insight into how their current function was related to their childhood constructions.

A symbolic character, however, might have experienced the therapist's statement "I am not your father" as helpful in a different way. A symbolic character might have, for example, used the intervention to help him with reality testing. Instead of having an insight into unconscious motivations, he could have taken the intervention as a reminder that he must practice distinguishing one person from another or that there was a limit to the closeness offered by his therapist. An intuitive character might find the intervention useful if he felt that the therapist was trying to teach him that obvious attempts at manipulation would not be successful. Thus the same intervention may be helpful to very different persons, but for different reasons. Of course, other patients would not experience that intervention as at all helpful. For example, one such patient might experience the interpretation as his being abandoned. Another, like Mr. B. (Chapter 9), might think the therapist was trying to humiliate him.

One should not expect that an intervention will always have the same effect even with the same individual. Clearly psychology deals with a difficult-to-manage and difficult-to-predict system.[27] Some of our colleagues have stopped trying to find consistency to an individual's behavior across situations. They resort to a "carrot and stick approach" to alter (and to explain) behavior. Obviously we belong to a different group, perhaps more naive, but somewhat more hopeful and more respectful of the concept of individual consistency. We believe it behooves us to attempt to understand how a particular patient will experience an intervention or at least to recognize how it has been experienced.

The therapist's interventions with the patient are of two kinds: (1) He provides an overall atmosphere or tone. We refer to this as the therapist's stance. (2) He offers "packets" of information, i.e., he attempts to communicate something (verbally and nonverbally) from time to time. The atmosphere and the attempts to communicate information may each be consistent or inconsistent over time. Either may be consistent or inconsistent with the other. Patient and therapist alike, being human, are not entirely consistent. Furthermore, as noted, what the patient makes of what the therapist does is a function of the patient. These factors all contribute to the difficulties in predicting the therapist–patient system, but there is, nonetheless, some correspondence between the intent of the therapist and the experience of the patient.

An alert therapist will modify his efforts as he notices clues as to how he is being perceived by the patient. For example, when Mr. B's assumption about placement of the ashtray by the therapist became a focus, Mr. B began to talk about leaving town. (After an intervention, it is often wise for the therapist to listen to his patient's next two paragraphs, the next two subjects. Usually within their themes is an indication of how the patient reads the therapist's intervention.) An alert therapist might wonder if the patient was considering changing therapists, or leaving therapy, and might then ask himself how or if this change might be averted.

Recognizing the variability inherent in patient and therapist, we will limit our discussion by assuming that the therapist's interventions are interpreted by the patient as the therapist intended, or, if they are not, as if the therapist recognizes and corrects any misconceptions the patient has. We may then consider how the intended results of interpretation, guidance, and management of attachment or merger affect the character structures.

What does insight do to each of the three character types? We proposed that insight is appropriate for the operational character. But what happens when insight is processed by the operational character? Since we have proposed a structuralist system, what happens to what structures? Good—well-timed, nonintellectualized, emotionally laden, in-the-transference, and/or worked-through—insight effects what kind of change in what kind of structure? We think insight in the operational produces what we term a formal operational correction, but not a change from one character structure to another.

For example, Mr. M automatically tended to expect others to be "out for his best interests" as he felt his father had been, or to expect that they should be. He expected that they would not compete with him, but might try to hold him back. After developing insight into such expectations, he monitored, modulated, and even laughed at his expectations some of the time, but the expectations persisted. Are not monitoring, modulating, and laughing at really examples of working through? We answer that working through is a kind of formal operational correction. The monitoring, the modulating, and the laughing at are corrections of the expectation. It is a thinking about thinking, what we term a formal operational correction in the social domain.

When Mr. M feigned illness to avoid a painful and useless business appointment, he used an intuitive style of function that was appropriate to a certain situation. For Mr. M, such deception required much conscious thought and was a small triumph of reason over his usual approach. Lying to avoid a commitment was an intuitive social cognitive correction of (his usual) operational social cognition. It is an example of intuitive thinking about operational thinking in the social domain. Mr. M had to decide that doing what he would like to do now should override his automatic honesty. He had to make a type of formal operational correction, i.e., to perform a type of second-order thinking. In this instance Mr. M successfully overcame those people who imposed on his time and felt triumphant over them (something an intuitive would do and feel without conflict) as well as feeling triumphant (although somewhat guilty) at defeating his own automatic tendency to keep his word.

Insight is the principle curative agent in treatment of the operational, and the most fundamental insight is insight into the transference. Any transference is a part of the patient's context, his view of the therapist, an attribute that is not a part of the therapist. Insight into the transference accordingly modifies or takes away a part of the context. The abstinent stance and transference interpretation (which is in keeping with the abstinent stance) both send the message: You are able to be on your own and you are on your own. Through this transference interpretation the self-representation is divided from object representation, but only in terms of function or who owns the self's function. An attribute of objects, self and object, is modified, but generally, as with Mr. M, the patient keeps doing as before, catching himself and adjusting his automatic responses.

For an intuitive character, insight into interactions or behaviors may be helpful as long as such insight is not damaging to the patient's self-esteem. Insight into his qualities, i.e., his need for narcissistic supplies or his impulsivity, may help if he does not view these characteristics as bad, but as something with which he must reckon. The reckoning is a form of formal operational correction. To the extent that it is experienced as criticism, interpretation will be rejected by the intuitive patient; if not, it may emphasize the dysfunctional and painful aspects of his behavior, causing discomfort without benefit. Intellectualized insight, however, may slow his impulsivity and enhance his self-esteem, a formal operational correction. Any insights into his interactions with people may be turned to his advantage. If he can understand other people's motives more clearly, he can use this understanding to get what he wants, again a formal operational correction.

What happens when insight is given to a symbolic character? In a symbolic, well-delivered, emotional insight may shatter further an already fragmented–merged (undifferentiated) conceptualization of the self and the world. Or insight may convert a depressed state into an acute paranoid one. One patient complained about her mistreatment at the hands of her employer, then talked about cutting out a pattern with a scissors. Her therapist, connecting the two themes, said, "I'd run a scissors through him [the employer]." The following day the patient fled from a car when she became overwhelmed by the fear that her driving companion would kill her. In such a case, insight affects the core of the symbolic, the character structure, but it does not change the basic quality of the core. It does not change the symbolic into an operational or an intuitive.

Somewhat intellectualized insight or defense-mobilizing insight may help a symbolic patient strengthen his ego boundaries. Sometimes such defensive maneuvers appear to involve the core character structure; at other times they only result in formal operational corrections. In either case we think that the lack of definition or threat of lack of definition of the core remains. Telling a symbolic patient that he jumps from part to whole or that he tends to over-attach, or inducing him to accept his bad self, helps him define himself and accordingly the external world. Sometimes he learns to catch himself making assumptions or attaching. Catching himself may help him to modify his behavior, to diversify attachments, or to limit closeness. He is reckoning with his proclivities, a thinking about thinking. Occasionally well-delivered, affect-laden insight is helpful, diminishing both anxiety and depression. In such instances the insight is less a new piece of knowledge ("Aha") than it is a sense of being understood and of not being alone.

LEARNING

We guide the intuitive. What does guidance do for him and what does it do for the other two character types?

We help the intuitive to get what he wants more effectively and without his getting into trouble. We take a more
kindly attitude toward greed, in him and in others, including ourselves, hoping he will take a more kindly attitude
toward his own greed. We teach and model, and he learns
and identifies. But he also feels watched out for, and as a
result, his self-esteem increases.

What happens in treatment of an intuitive character is
parallel in form to what happens in treatment of an operational, because, like the operational, the intuitive is certain
of who he is and of what the world is like. Although the
views of the intuitive and the operational are very different, they are settled, unlike those of the symbolic. (As the
operational tends to think the world is peopled by operationals or should be, the intuitive thinks the world is peopled by intuitives or should be.) The guidance is directed
at helping an intuitive to deal more effectively with others.
He considers the various possibilities available in a relationship with another and tries to choose the possibility
most likely to work for him. He may learn to sense the
other person's investment or state and to know when to
close a deal or when to compromise. Through identification or imitation, and by picking up tips, he learns to delay
a bit for a better payoff. By identifying with the therapist's
attitude toward selfish pursuits, an intuitive may become
more tolerant of his own selfish strivings, and thus may
have less need to deny or to project. The core character
structure may thus be softened, but the intuitive does not
become an operational or a symbolic, and most of the
change is in the area of formal operations.

What about guiding an operational? To the extent the
operational character is guided, he may improve his handling of situations and may feel taken care of or controlled.
But perceiving others in the same old ways, he may not
function as well as he could and may in the long run be
more anxious and have lower self-esteem than he might
were he getting insight instead of guidance.

Guidance should be helpful to the symbolic if he can use the advice and if he feels appropriately connected to the therapist and defined, not usurped or alienated by being led.

ATTACHMENT AND MERGER

In the symbolic character we titrate attachment and merger, hence identity of self and objects. In correct measure, the connection itself defines, values, and provides a sense of belonging and safety. A symbolic may learn to limit his attachments or to diversify them. He may use interventions to define himself and to bolster his self-esteem. Chants such as "I am unique," "I am bright, that's why I don't fit in," or an opposite chant in a particular symbolic—"We are all one"—define and value.

We think that in the symbolic's development any maturational closure takes place on nonunitary, i.e., overlapping and incomplete, sets belonging to the self and the outside, so that self and object are poorly defined. In treatment, this lack of definition may allow the therapist access to the core, i.e., access to part objects including the patient's part self. Some of these part objects are nonlogically merged. Support by the therapist of a part allows for better definition, hence direction, and enhanced self-esteem. Better definition and enhanced self-esteem improve function and often each thrives on the other, just as in decompensation loss of one tends to erode the other.

We generally protect the symbolic's defenses, when not too distorting, because they provide organization and often help spare anxiety or depression. Ms. D's (Chapter 9) characterization of herself as "vulnerable to stress" offered her greater definition and direction but could have damaged her self-esteem. Yet if she values considerateness and kindliness and if the easygoing motherly atmosphere was seen as more positive than the hard-driving corporate world, then "vulnerable to stress" might also support her self-worth.

We think conversion-like experience is successful with symbolics. Yochelson and Samenow's (1976) approach, Alcoholics Anonymous, fundamental Protestantism, and even certain cults may provide this experience. The symbolic patient or member benefits by incorporating a "new" identity, sometimes even a "bad" one. This new identity may enhance his self-esteem (as he feels he is a true Christian or a recovering alcoholic), and may justify derision of the outside world. Embracing a role defines his self and his morals, and provides goals: "I am a Christian," "a healer," "a criminal," "a dope fiend," or "an alcoholic." (Sometimes a negatively valued self may provide an internal equilibrium, with self-condemnation dealing with unjustified angry impulses that would be directed toward others.) The basic core configuration still persists, with part of self projected outward. After he becomes converted, the convert distances himself from his part, e.g., his angry or greedy impulses, which is now seen as belonging to the unconverted, the nonalcoholic, or the outsider. Although more completely defined by such a conversion, the symbolic is still a symbolic, and his identity is often an uncomfortable one. A negative identity, e.g., as a dope fiend, is often unstable. The burden of always being Christian or always being therapeutic is heavy. The symbolic has, however, dealt with his core configuration; he has found an identity.

What happens when the therapist offers merger to an operational character? The operational should not be able to merge with the therapist except in the area of function. Such merger should have the same effect as guiding. Merger with the intuitive character should also not be possible, although the caring and valuing aspect of the relationship should enhance self-esteem. An intuitive might also become suspicious of a therapist who offers merger.

Chapter 14

A STRUCTURAL APPROACH
TO CHANGE
Metapsychological Comments

COGNITIVE MECHANISMS FOR CHANGE

In the cognitive domain the mechanisms for change are identification or imitation, alteration of defenses or coping, and know-how or insight. That is, style of organization of information may be altered or information may be added (or both). Each of these mechanisms lies on a continuum extending from unconscious to conscious,[28] with identification, defenses, and know-how at the unconscious end of the continuum and imitation, coping, and insight at the conscious end of the continuum.[29]

We may deliberately attempt to induce a patient to model himself after the therapist. We may take a considerate, understanding attitude toward someone who has mistreated our intuitive patient and at the same time invite the patient to wonder why that person, the persecutor, would act in such a manner (see Chapter 10, p. 163–164). As noted, because an intuitive character tends to externalize and to project, we may expect that his resentments about his persecutor reflect parts of himself for which he has little tolerance. We hope that if the patient can identify with our more tolerant attitude toward the persecutor, then the patient can take a more tolerant view of himself and his similar bad behavior. He will then not have to flee from his own self-condemnation through the use of acting out, projection, and externalization or denial. This modification may take place consciously or unconsciously. Aside from its impact on defenses, the patient's identification with the therapist's attitude impacts affect, reducing the intensity of depression, shame, self-condemnation, or anger. Thus change begins in one area of cognition, but affects other cognitive areas and the affects as well.

When an operational patient wonders why he is so angry at a person who is breaking the rules, he may recognize that he too would like to break the same rules but is fearful or would feel guilty and therefore does not dare. Insight undermines his defensive projection of his anger, and there is a shift in cognition. He is no longer focused on the rules and their violation but on his envy of the daring rule breaker or on his own timidity. His affect also shifts as a function of this shift in cognitive foci.

Not only may we intervene at different points in the patient's psychological system to effect change, but an intervention in one domain often affects other domains. Use of mood-altering drugs that presumably act only on affects may result in cognitive change as well. These interactions may help explain why approaches with different intentions sometimes have similar results or vice versa, especially since the patient's systems are the final common pathways to his thought, feeling, or behavior. As change occurs, defenses[30] may seem to loosen, dissolve, or build up, or there may be a swapping of defenses. Changes in defensive operations may be general or they may involve only one or a few defenses.

Defense mechanisms such as repression, projection, and displacement are unconscious, each with corresponding conscious mechanisms such as suppression, blaming, and finding a distraction. The more unconscious the agent of change, the more automatic and lasting the change tends to be. Among the defense mechanisms, identification is the most significant modifier and reorganizer, for learning or for defense. Identification and incorporation take data in, while the other defenses tend to set data (experience) aside. Presumably all types of defenses assign the aliment to existing schemes as a function of affect, affect directing and signaling the quality of fit of the aliment into existing schemes. These shifts in patterns of activity account for refinement of structure of both the social-ego and presumably the thing-ego; these patterns work better, but are not necessarily patterns that reflect rigorous logic.

METAPSYCHOLOGIC CONSIDERATIONS OF AFFECT

Affect and cognition never occur entirely separately, but they are physically and psychologically distinct. Affect and cognition presumably correspond to activities in distinct, although interconnecting, subunits of the brain. The somatic therapies tend to support this assumption. Electroconvulsive therapy, antidepressants, and antianxiety medication appear to act directly on affect systems and only secondarily on cognition. Particular social interactions will have a primarily affective conscious response, whether it is humiliation, depression, or joy, whereas other interactions will result mainly in new thoughts and perceptions, or will bring to mind past ideas.

Although nontrivial behavior cannot change without either cognitive or affective change as a prior cause, any or all components of affect or cognition may be unconscious. While affect or cognition may or may not be manifest in behavior, changes in behavior when manifest may enable us to infer an unconscious mechanism. A symptom such as a conversion reaction, which stands in lieu of thoughts and emotion, supports our invoking Freud's concept of a dynamic unconscious. A person may be unaware either of his behavior change or of its cause. A person may appear depressed to his friends and only become aware of his depression when told about his appearance.

According to Inhelder and Piaget (1958), psychological structure depends on neural maturation, interaction with the physical environment, and influence of the social milieu. The form the structure takes is a function of its adaptation by equilibrium with the social and physical environment. In their view the psychological structures that persist and repeat are those that have been adaptive to social and physical conditions, those that have worked well as the person interacted with his milieu. In such a system every change is a re-equilibration, since we are not just a collection of unrelated parts (although sometimes the re-equilibration involves compartmentalization, i.e., organizing schemes as if they were isolated parts). The organism, using the structures that it already has with their inherent interconnections, will tend toward adaptation. We believe this adaptation is monitored by affect (Malerstein & Ahern, 1982). Affect is a rough index of adaptation, of what works and what does not and how it works. There are three classes of conscious affect, none precisely separate from the other: (1) the group that signals the state of the body, e.g., hunger, fatigue, and sexual arousal, (2) another that signals the state of the organisms's interaction with the outside world, e.g., fear, love, and hate, and (3) one that signals the state of the psyche, e.g., anxiety, elation, and depression. Presumably each conscious affect is a manifestation of affective activity that is nonconscious. We, like Wexler (1986), subscribe to Luria's notion "that the neural substances of emotion are those processes that integrate different brain regions"

(p. 357). Like Pugh (Pugh, 1977; Brown & Weiss, 1982), and not unlike Piaget (1981a), we think of the positive and negative affects, sometimes experienced as emotions, i.e., sometimes conscious, as the index of what works for a particular psychological structure, a rough guide for a given set of activities. In a way all we know about how well we are doing—all we adapt to—is our own affects.

We think that anxiety and depression as symptoms are not bound to any one character type. There appears to be a sequence of development of emotions, as of cognitive stages: depression appears before humiliation, and humiliation before guilt (Malerstein, 1968). There is an intertwining of social cognitive development with the affective sequence, just as there are ties connecting certain affects to certain social cognitive structures. For example, humiliation is integral to, and frequently expressed in, intuitive characters, whereas guilt is integral to, and frequently expressed in, operational characters. The more severe phobias—panics and panphobias—are usually found in symbolics. The obsessive–compulsive persons who manifest agitated depressions when they are facing the downhill side of life—patients we used to diagnose as involutional depressives or paranoids—generally prove to be operational symbolics.

METAPSYCHOLOGIC CONSIDERATIONS OF COGNITIVE STRUCTURE

When discussing psychotherapy we talk about changes in structure and changes in content. A change in structure is generally judged to be more significant and to imply lasting change, whereas a change in content is thought to be less important and less lasting. In the theory of therapy we propose, structure is paramount. But what is structure and what is content? What is their relationship to each other?

Piaget (1971) defined structure as a wholeness, a system that has its own laws of transformation and in this sense is self-regulating. During any transformation some parts of the system must remain stable. A structure may have relationships with other structures. The set of whole numbers is a structure that is a substructure of the set of real numbers. A kidney cell is part of a kidney tubule that in turn is part of a kidney.

Russell's (1948) definition of structure is not greatly different from that of Piaget. Russell defined structure as the parts and their interrelationships. He dealt with individuation or particulateness of structure by adopting Liebniz's solution that "a particular is constituted by qualities; when all its qualities are enumerated, it is fully defined" (p. 292). Russell was interested in defining individuation of structure as a universal in time and space. To define an instance in time and space, i.e., an individual structure, he invoked the notion of a complete complex of compresence. For example, if one sees something and hears something else at the same time the interrelationship is compresence. One may, at the same time feel, anticipate, or remember something; all these form a complex of compresence. Such a complex is complete if one goes on until nothing further is "compresent with each and all the members of the group" (p. 294). If part A is compresent with part B then the structure is incomplete without part B. If a part is compresent with some part that is outside the interrelated parts as conceived, then the structure is incomplete; the outside part somehow belongs to the structure. Without limits or bounds to structure, one cannot deal with events, order, or cause.

When we refer to relationships of one structure to another, we are noting individuation and boundaries of structures. The structure of a cell has a lipid membrane that serves as a border of the structure and as an interface between itself and other structures, including aliment. The border, the cell membrane, is a part of the structure, a part of the cell. If it breaks the structure is lost.

In a psychological structure, such as a scheme, a talent, or a dialect, with its corresponding neural patterns, what constitutes the boundary? Does it have a cell membrane? How similar are psychological structures or schemes— neural patterns that repeat and generalize—to cells or to the set of whole numbers?

Certainly some psychological structures are abiding: they repeat and they generalize. Diligence or talent in mathematics, in science, in reading, in listening, in language, in mothering, or in having fun, any of which may be characterized as schemes, are each in some measure distinct from one another within one person. What accounts for the coherence and boundedness of psychological structures? Is coherence of structure situation-determined as behaviorists would say? Is the situation a "cell membrane" that gives shape and boundedness to whatever is going on in the person? Must we include the external situation as part of the psychological structure? Certainly under some conditions, the external situation is very important. Milgram's (1963) experiments, in which most subjects were induced to (pseudo) torture students, and Schachter and Singer's (1971) work, in which an injected drug was experienced differently depending on external circumstances, imply that the external situation may be crucial. Even Goedel's (Piaget, 1971) theorem that there can be no proof of a system solely from within the system suggests that no system can be defined solely from within. Nevertheless, there is evidence for some kind of internal "wiring," patterns that may be accessed, or configurations that bear their owner's mark. Some people did not volunteer for the Milgram experiment, and others withdrew. It is difficult to dismiss the fact that certain chemicals depress, others calm, whereas still others elate, and that there appears to be some kind of specific pattern to the brain's response. Situation is not everything.

Following Russell's (1948) proposal that structure is the parts plus the relationships between those parts, content of a structure is its parts plus their relationships. So content, if we consider the total content, is the same as structure. But what about the fact that we say one structure is different from another structure? Here we are talking about the boundary of a structure. But a boundary of a structure is a part of the structure; boundary is a piece of content. So we still have a structure as equivalent to the sum of its parts and their relationships. Structure is thus coincident with its content.

If we now start to discuss a visual object scheme as a structure, perhaps we can answer the question of what is a psychologic structure and what are its boundaries. As argued by the second author, a child first shows evidence of discrimination of one visual object scheme from another following upon the myelination of the geniculocalcarine tract to the specific visual sensory apparatus of his brain, area 17 of the occipital lobe of the cerebral cortex (Malerstein, 1986). The function of area 17 of the brain is the categorization of incoming visual neural activity in accordance with its correspondence to lines and edges of light, particularly edges of light that move as a set as they impact upon the retina. Edges or lines of light that move as a set are the single most distinctive criterion for distinguishing one visual object from another. It is not likely that in the brain the separateness of one object representative from another is demarcated by some kind of shell or closed set of "edges" of neural activity that surrounds the content of each object representation. Rather, as part of the neural activity corresponding to watching an object, as part of that total content, the particular content that corresponds to edges moving as a set weighs most heavily in specifying whether a pattern of activity is one that corresponds to a separate object. The edge-movement organization of visual activity is not the only important function that lends itself to construction of visual objects as separate from each other. For example, differences in coloration of two objects also help to distinguish them. Edge-movement organization of visual data is, however, the most salient feature that may be used in any construction to distinguish one visual object from another.

Ultimately, an object, instance, or individual is the "compresence" of many factors none of which are outside of it (Russell, 1948). This is the essence of individuation or separateness of one thing from another. Russell pointed out, however, that we can perceive a particular complex (a structure) without perceiving all of its components. In other words, it is not required that all of the parts of a scheme be active in order for us to know that the scheme is active. (We do not have to see or imagine all of a person's parts to know he is there or to think about him.)

We suggest that Russell's definition of individual structure omits the fact that some parts of a structure, some contents, have a greater valence than others. In an adaptive organism some parts of a structure are more critical in marking that structure's operation. Consider that the single most reliable visual index of a separate object is that its edges move as a set. Then when the infant's efforts are to grasp all objects he sees and bring them to his mouth, on balance, if he attempts to grasp a spectacle (to him a spectacle, to the adult or older child an object) whose visual edges move as a set, he is more likely to bring that spectacle to his mouth than if he used some other visual index (of objects), e.g., color or brightness differences. There comes a time when we see and understand the world in terms of sets of edges that do not interpenetrate each other, solid objects that may not occupy the same space but may go behind one another or lie on top of one another. So line/edge-movement is exploited and as a component of visual objectness works best. Patches of dark or light, or color are not as reliable indicators of separate objects, although they work some of the time.

Our point is that while a structure is the sum of its parts and their relationships, some of the parts and their relationships virtually define the structure. Some parts of a structure have a higher valence or carry a higher level of confidence. The boundedness of the psychological structure that defines an object is not like a cell membrane, but is just one or several salient components.

Furthermore, depending on the use one has for a particular substructure, it may be defined by a different part or combination of parts. Aside from its neural substructure[32] we suggest that what gives shape and distinction to a psychological structure are its salient parts. When we perceive a person it is not that his picture, his shape contained by his skin, is transmitted back via the optic radiations to the occipital lobe where a little man looks at it. Rather there is transmission of lines and edges of light and their movement as a set relatively specifically located cell in area 17, hence distinctive location of impulse patterns beyond area 17 further into the brain. From this pattern, along with other components, e.g., lack of penetrability of lines and edges, objectness is constructed. One "learns" that things work better if one understands that something with continuous edges that move as a set and are impenetrable (1) is separate and different from random activity, (2) is separate and different from other sets of activity that correspond to past objects that have no current perceptive component and, (3) is separate and different from other sets of edges that are compresent. Eventually only certain patterns of sets of edges will go together with reaching, grasping, and "suckability," e.g., a wooden block. Other patterns will go together with "petability" or "bitability," e.g., a dog.

We propose that character structure persists: once an intuitive, always an intuitive; once an operational, always an operational; and once a symbolic, always a symbolic. How can we account for such stability of psychological structure? We observe that in adults the configuration of qualities we call character structure, like any scheme, abides over time and in varying situations. Clinical work has ascribed similar fixity to personality structure. There is a certain fixity to a French or an English accent. For most of us it is very hard to learn a new language after age 12 without some residual accent. Obviously none of this is without exception, but these psychological configurations generally fix, and we wonder why. What gives the structure cohesiveness, what bounds it, what is its membrane? And what gives it stability?

If what limits and makes distinctive a psychic structure is not some hard shell around content but rather some particular pieces of content, then those pieces of content should be changeable as is any other piece of content. However, if a part is salient, then that suggests it would have more interrelationships and more important interrelationships with other parts or contents, and thus would be harder to change. In addition, if you change a salient part you may destroy, seriously damage, or redefine that structure. We have also proposed that the stability of older structures may be supported by subsequent maturational reorganizations that preclude former ways of accessing the old structure (Malerstein, 1986). Once we have an edge-organizing function in the visual system most new data are expected to be organized differently. All of those earlier, less-differentiated patterns of central activity will still be there, subject to activation, and will be compresent as "memories," but they will be accessed primarily in accordance with the new styles of data handling.[33] That is, in the visual system they will be accessed peripherally only by configurations of activity corresponding to lines and edges of light.

In the visual system, the combinations of motor or sensory activity that gain access to this more diffusely organized central system will be more limited than before. There will still be some freedom within this more primitive organization, with some potential even for chance operation, and even some likelihood of older, more diffuse operation, but exit and entry points will tend to be restricted by what seems to work best, when such aids as line/edge-movement gates are available.[34]

We are not suggesting that maturation is the defining part of structure, but rather that maturation provides a tool for constructing structures of a new type. Maturation also tends to restrict access by the old avenues to the old structures. Yet once accessed, the less-differentiated configurations still have power. We assume that this takes place in the concrete operational period and the formal operational period, with maturational changes inducing cognitive reorganization that limits access, therapeutic or nontherapeutic, to the more primitive systems.

We don't know what organic factor(s) induce the ability to classify or seriate values or attributes of objects, a defining capacity characteristic of the concrete operational period. Nor do we know what organic development lends itself to seeking possible exceptions to classifications or orderings, the distinguishing characteristic of formal operational cognition. Nonetheless we anticipate that such organic inductors will be found. We think one's sense of self and of others and even one's style of talking may be held in place by the interface between the newer system and the old one, the old one stable and automatic, the new one somewhat flexible and fluid, the new one serving the old, the old one tending to be less conscious (Malerstein, 1986).

The thinker, the latency-age child, who decided that he was a person deserving of good things, and that social beings and their rules are trustworthy, has an organization that holds together and seems to work reasonably well in his world. Consider also the child whose interaction with his social world has enabled him to understand the world as a jungle and to acquire the know-how to operate in that world. His understanding and know-how also work well for him in that world. Later, in adolescence, each child notes exceptions, i.e., practices formal operations, but these exceptions do not appear to change his basic sense of himself and the world. [We wonder, but do not know, if the symbolic with uncertainties about his boundaries and those of the world does not find adolescence (with its introduction of exceptions and limitless possibilities) more confusing than do the other two character types. Might this be an avenue of investigation in understanding schizophrenia? Bohart and Henschel (1984) have considered this question.]

At some point maturation induces the adolescent to consider many possibilities, i.e., to use formal operational cognition. This reorganization perhaps closes off those systems he used to construct his view of the world either as a park or as a jungle. A child in the concrete operational period somehow tends to arrive at a single answer that coordinates any apparent discrepancies as he constructs his understanding of attributes such as morality or color, whereas the child in the formal operational period entertains possibilities, looking for hypothetical exceptions. This latter child has already decided what is moral; he may know that everyone should be trustworthy, or on the contrary, he may know that everyone is out to get what they can. One of these principles served him well in his social world. However, if he believed that everyone including himself should be trustworthy, in adolescence he starts to wonder if there are circumstances where one should be dishonest. Or if he believed that you'd better "get what you can whenever you can," he wonders if there are times when sacrificing something now will lead to greater getting. If this latter adolescent is offered new aliment—if it is said to him or shown to him that his definition of the social world as a jungle is false and that the world is a park or that it is chaotic—he knows he is either dreaming or watching a movie: "It is not the real world." The heavily valenced parts of his structure of the social world, i.e., his interactions with social beings, do not fit with this other aliment. Any such new aliment belongs to another space, perhaps to history, to the future, to art, to hallucination, to sleight of hand, or, at least, to the hypothetical.

Our points are that structure is content, but that some types of content are more important than others, and that those parts define the structure more than does other content. Also, subsequent reorganization may be the factor that makes these earlier structures largely unalterable.[35]

Chapter 15

RECENT FINDINGS IN
DEVELOPMENTAL PSYCHOLOGY

We think Piaget's system is a general psychology, a constructivist–interactionist–digestive model that lends itself to understanding the relationships of mind and brain, of normal and abnormal, and of adult and child. In our first book (Malerstein & Ahern, 1982) we drew upon Piaget's work and on clinical findings to explain character structure formation. Malerstein (1986) employed Piaget's constructs and findings to explain consciousness, and then combined these with neurophysiologic (Hubel & Weisel, 1979), and neuroanatomic (Lecours, 1975) findings to show how brain maturation could induce cognitive stage reorganization. In this book we demonstrate how we apply our Piagetian model of character structure in the clinical setting.

Some developmental psychology findings have been presented as basic challenges to Piaget's work (Stern, 1985; Meltzoff & Moore, 1977). In our previous works, not having recognized the consistency and significance of these findings, we did not address them. Because we propose that Piaget's psychology is a general one, we feel compelled to discuss these new findings here.

Recent findings suggest that children achieve developmental milestones earlier than reported by Piaget. They also emphasize maturational factors as instrumental to development. We find no basic conflict between these findings and the fundamental aspects of Piaget's system. The Piagetian system accommodates these new findings without serious damage, although the new findings do mandate several alterations of his concepts just as clinical material suggested certain modifications in the Piagetian system (Malerstein & Ahern, 1982).

The new findings in child development that we will deal with first suggest that the child is prewired for certain functions, such as imitation, in ways Piaget could not have known when he first formulated his ideas. Later in this chapter we will discuss a different genre of recent findings, attachment studies.

Stern (1985) along with Meltzoff and Moore (1977) proposed that the occurrence of certain early imitative behavior undermines Piaget's concept that imitation or representation must be constructed by the child in steps. They view both imitation and representation as innate, and not constructed as Piaget proposed.

When imitating facial gestures the child is not able to see his own facial movement, and thus such imitation had been assumed to be difficult to learn. According to Piaget (1962), a 6- to 8-month-old child first imitates a model sticking out his tongue only if the child has an index scheme, e.g., a sound such as the bubbling noise of saliva, to connect to or assimilate to the protrusion of his own tongue. A child may imitate the model's opening his mouth when the index is the feeding situation. According to Piaget it is not until about 9 months of age that a child can without benefit of an index scheme imitate facial gestures he cannot see.

Early imitation was first observed by a Piagetian, Maratos (Stern, 1985), who reported that children as young as

2 weeks of age may imitate an experimenter's sticking his tongue out. It was subsequently corroborated, systematized, and extended to another activity, mouth opening, by Meltzoff and Moore (1977). Further support for early imitation capacity is the report by Field, Woodson, Greenberg, and Cohen (1982) that 2-day-old children imitate smiles, frowns, and expressions of surprise. This imitation takes place much earlier than Piaget reported. Such imitation of facial movements must somehow involve a built-in cross-connection of visual configurations of activity with tactile and proprioceptive configurations of activity.

In addition to these early imitations, other findings imply prewiring of the touch and proprioceptive systems to the visual system. A blindfolded 3-week-old child, allowed to suck on a nubby nipple, stared longer at a nubby nipple than he did at a smooth nipple when the blindfold was removed (Meltzoff & Borton, 1979). The irregularity of tactile and proprioceptive activation corresponding to nubbiness must somehow be related to the irregularity of visual activity corresponding to nubbiness. At this early age, however, it is not likely that a child understands that he is touching nubbiness with his tongue or that he is seeing nubbiness, since he has as yet no concept of touching or seeing. Therefore it is understood that these responses are amodal, not cross-modal (Stern, 1985), although they do reflect patterned cross-connecting of sensory and motor regions.

Other experiments are also consonant with amodal prewiring. Using decreased heart rate as a measure of habituation, researchers found that a child will habituate to a particular temporal correspondence of visual and auditory patterns of activity, whether that correspondence is in duration, beat, or rhythm (Allen, Walker, Symonds, & Marcell, 1977; Demany et al., 1977; Humphrey, Tees, & Werker, 1979; Stern, 1985). For example if a light is flashed at a certain frequency, initially the child's heart rate accelerates. After a while the child habituates to the stimulus: that is, the heart rate returns to normal. Subsequently if sounds are made at the same frequency as the flashes, the child's heart rate continues at its normal frequency. Without earlier habituation, however, the child's heart rate increases when the sounds are introduced. The child manifests amodal habituation to frequency of activation.

Aside from amodal sensitivity being prewired, some special sensitivities in the person domain appear to be built-in. A 3-day-old child turns his head to the breast pad of his mother rather than to the breast pad of a stranger (MacFarlane, 1975). A newborn child will suck more if his sucking movement (through electronic hookups) causes a recording of his mother's voice to play (Siqueland & De-Lucia, 1969). Infants prefer to look at faces rather than at other visual configurations (Fantz, 1963). Six-week-old children look more at faces that speak than at faces in which lip movement is not synchronized with sound (Haith, 1980). If 3-month-olds are exposed for 2 minutes to movies and soundtracks of rotating transparent containers filled with either a single object or multiple objects, then after a 3-minute delay they look at rotating containers whose sounds are synchronous rather than at containers whose sounds are not (Bahrick, 1988). Association of sounds that were asynchronous with rotation of the containers does not take place.

Stern (1985) drew on such findings of early amodal connections to infer that motivated imitation and representation occur much earlier than suggested by Piaget and that they need not be constructed, but that they are prewired. In our opinion the new findings do not demonstrate that the child is capable of representation from the outset, nor that imitations at a later age are simply continuous with imitations at 3 weeks of age, nor that these later imitations need not be constructed. The new findings suggest to us 2 things: (1) The undifferentiation of the brain is profound; different entry ports, e.g., vision and proprioception (and the exit ports, i.e., the motor systems), are interconnected in the newborn. This is in keeping with our understanding of the scheme: the sucking scheme, for example, is much more than just sucking activity (Malerstein & Ahern, 1982; Malerstein, 1986).[36] The sucking scheme is not just sensorimotor activity in the touch and proprioceptive systems, but includes position sense, taste, satiation, warmth from an adjacent body, ambient lighting, sounds, and so on. (2) Both amodal responsiveness of the organism engaged in imitation and amodal habituation to activation patterns (duration, beat, rhythm, and intensity) suggest that the cross-connections of brain regions are configuration-sensitive. That is, global categorization of brain activity in terms of duration, beat, rhythm, and intensity is present at birth. Interestingly, Piaget (1962) reported amodal or cross-modal behavior when he wrote that L. at 11 months imitated the experimenter's eye blinking by opening and closing his fist or his mouth. This observation points again to an amodal or cross-modal configuration sensitivity of brain activity.

It is of note that one must be very precise in order to elicit early imitation and that this imitation tends to fade (Inhelder, personal communication). In addition, a child will not only imitate a person's sticking out his tongue but also will respond by sticking his tongue out when the person protrudes a pencil from his hand (Stern, 1985). Thus the child need not have any representation of his imitation of another person's sticking out his tongue; he is simply prewired to be configuration-sensitive. In some way motor protrusion is connected to visual protrusion.

Such amodal activities provide evidence of certain built-in systems of connections and constraints in the central nervous system that are not always obvious. It seems likely that this prewiring later lends itself to the construction of the cross-modal patterning involved in deliberate imitation (Maratos, 1982). This prewiring is parallel to the wiring of the visual system's area 17 as a line-edge gate (Hubel & Weisel, 1979; Malerstein, 1986). Any prewired configuration sensitivity provides some early definition of the schemes that may be built upon, just as reflexes, schemes such as sucking or grasping, may be built upon [as described by Piaget (1954)].

Evidence for early definition of person schemes follows from findings that the organism has prewired tendencies to select persons by smell differentiation, preference for facial configurations, and preference for visual lip movement that corresponds to the sounds being heard. These prewirings foster separation of persons from things, hence to some degree of social from physical. Although both the social and physical worlds must be constructed by the child, such built-in scheme definition gives the child an advantage when constructing in the social domain as opposed to the physical domain, and when differentiating the social domain from the physical domain.

ATTACHMENT EXPERIMENTS

Bowlby, an ethologically oriented psychoanalyst, has drawn our attention to attachment being at least as important as feeding and mating (Main, 1987). He proposed that along with other ground-living primates, humans (beginning at about 1 year of age) automatically track their lifelong physical and psychological access to a protective figure; this tracking aids in protection from predators, helps to maintain body temperature, and facilitates the organism's ability to eat, drink, and keep up with the troop. Attachment is essential to survival. "Exploration is a luxury" (Main, 1987).

Ainsworth's (1982) strange-situation provided an experimental paradigm to test Bowlby's clinical conceptualizations. In the strange-situation a mother brings her 1-year-old child into a room. A stranger enters. Mother leaves, returns, then leaves and returns, all during the course of 20 minutes. Children were classified by Ainsworth as A, B, or C babies. The majority of babies were B babies, babies who had secure attachments. They continued to explore the environment while their mothers were gone. When their mothers returned, they went to their mothers and then explored some more. Their behavior supported Bowlby's concepts. But Ainsworth was also interested in the babies who did not show the usual attachment behavior. Avoidant babies—A babies—ignored their mother's absence and shunned their mothers upon their return. Studies of heart rate indicated that these children were acutely aware of mother's return and departure, although their behavior did not show it. C babies—ambivalent babies—were increasingly inconsolable; they could not settle down when their mothers left, and were increasingly distressed at the second departure and return. These babies' behavioral classifications generally remained unchanged at age 18–20 months unless the mother's life situation changed.

Ainsworth found that mothers of As were rejecting of attachment behavior; mothers of Bs were accepting of attachment, sensitive, and responsive; and mothers of Cs were inconsistent in their attitudes toward attachment.

There is evidence that the A, B, and C individuals have distinctive behavior patterns at 6 years of age (Main, 1987): A individuals were aggressive, hostile, and detached; B children were better adjusted emotionally and socially; C children were anxious and victims of bullying. The 6 year olds' drawings, the way they talked, and transcripts of their verbal interactions with their mothers, as well as the way the mothers described their attachments to their own parents, were distinctive for each type. Generally a mother of an A child had problems remembering her own relationship to her parents. She tended to idealize the relationship, but when she recounted specific memories, these memories suggested that her parents were unavailable or not particularly concerned about her. A mother of a B child in describing her parents was fluent and coherent. Such a mother might have had a hard life: if so, she was clear about it and could explain it. A mother of a C child was preoccupied with the past. There was a lack of coherence in her stories about her parents, and often, the past intruded into the present as she spoke.

There were also babies whose behavior was difficult to classify as either A, B, or C. Main (1987) called these D babies, disoriented or disorganized. The mothers of D babies were frightened or frightening, and the babies seemed to be solutionless in that they could neither cling nor avoid when mother returned. One hid under a table. Another stopped in his tracks. A third put his head to the wall. Their drawings at 6 years of age were odd for 6 year olds. At this age they also tended to mother or boss their mothers.

Bowlby sees the child as forming a working model of the self and of the world, based on his interaction beginning at age 1 with his caregiver. This scheme according to Main (1987) is no different from Mandler's event representation or Piaget's scheme. It is also clear that Bowlby (1988) does not view A or C babies as predestined to become psychiatrically ill. He presented charts showing how A or C babies may take a number of different pathways toward normality. But a few such babies will be vulnerable to an adverse experience, such as a death in the family or a troublesome peer, which may cause them to deviate from the normal path, and to other experiences, such as a relationship with a helpful teacher or psychotherapist, that help them move closer to the normal path. Bowlby does not note as we would that B babies might also have their pathways to health, and vulnerabilities to pathology. This, however, is not a significant conflict between our concepts and his. Bowlby's branching style of development fits well with ours and with the kinds of formulations we think are necessary in order to deal with complex systems (see note 27).

We see a parallel between attachment theory and the related findings and our own theory of character structure. Except in level of abstraction there is not much difference between a sense of secure attachment and a sense of someone looking out for one's best interests. Thus if the quality of interaction between parent and child does not change greatly as the child passes from age 1 to age 7, then we would expect some consistency between A, B, C, and D types and our character structures. Certainly our notions of being looked out for (operational), of not being looked out for (intuitive), and of having certain prerequisites fulfilled before being looked out for (symbolic) seem to correspond to Ainsworth's descriptions of the behavior of mothers of B, A, and C children, respectively. Perhaps the mother's requirements for a D baby were too unpredictable, too confusing, for that particular child. To take into account our operational symbolics, intuitive symbolics, and mixed symbolics, however, we propose a complex classification. We speculate that some of the A babies are future intuitive symbolics, whereas some of the B babies are future operational symbolics. C and D babies are expected to become either pure or mixed symbolics.

Bowlby's concepts and findings, the strange-situation behaviors, and our clinical observations may be natural partners. We characterize symbolics as interested in attachment, and we also think that most adults are symbolics. Thus we also find, as Bowlby does, a need for attachment in adults [as does Kohut (Baker & Baker, 1987)]. We also postulate, however, that other adults, the pure operationals and intuitives, are not particularly attuned to attachment, although obviously none of us gets along completely on his own. Without a longitudinal study, we cannot be sure that Bowlby's attachment findings and our adult character structure are linked as we suggest, but the parallels are promising.

Piaget's theory appears to be a suitable general psychology. New findings of amodal and person-versus-thing prewiring as well as attachment theory do not invalidate Piaget's constructivist–interactionist–digestive model: they may be integrated into his model as may clinical observations of character structure. In the course of this integration certain components of Piaget's theory will be modified, but thus far the basic structure of his theory continues to be recognizable. Piaget's scheme accommodates without losing its identity.

Chapter 16

EPILOGUE

In our opinion any general theory of psychology must deal with the various psychiatric syndromes and with some of the findings of psychoanalysis, despite the fact that organized American psychiatry, as exemplified by its diagnostic manuals DSM-III and DSM-III-R, has minimized both. In our earlier books and in this book we proposed that Piaget's structural theory is superior to Freud's energic theory. We suggested that Piaget's stages of restructuring may account for certain broad options in character structure organization. We speculated how our character structures may relate to the agitated depressive syndrome (involutional melancholia) as well as to different personality configurations. Piaget (1962) attempted to deal with infantile sexuality, transference phenomena, dream analysis, and so on. We think his suggestions have considerable merit, but we would substitute "social structures" or "structures in the social domain" (which are necessarily more affectively laden than those in the physical domain) for his term "affective structures."

Many of the findings of psychoanalysis continue to be useful, although not universal. The child's belief in castration as an explanation of sexual differences certainly holds true for some children. Toilet training interaction as a basis for personality traits, and the oedipal complex, with its relationship to gender identity and object choice, retain importance. Of considerable appeal is Erickson's (1950) concept that culture feeds through the parents in their ministrations to their children to raise children that fit the culture. Keller (1978) integrated psychoanalytic and Piagetian concepts of object development with Western society's view of objectivity (rigorous separation of subject and object) and masculinity, showing them to be equivalent to each other and highly valued. As a result she cast light on the genderization of science and most importantly offered a model for gender-identity formation. We are especially concerned that the findings of dynamic psychiatry and the hard-won descriptions of clinical syndromes not be lost. Nonetheless we must leave further discussion of these for the future.

Our major effort in this book has been to illustrate how we apply our theory of character structure, a theory that grew out of clinical work but was shaped by Piaget's theory and findings. Our approaches, although perhaps not mainstream, are not essentially original. They are distillations of our selections of the literature and our experience with patients. Our theory is an organizing system that helps us to understand patients, choose basic goals for a patient, and style our interventions toward achieving those goals. We hope we have helped the reader along these same lines.

NOTES

1. See Waldinger's (1987) article on intensive treatment of the borderline. He reports that patients self-select therapeutic approaches, i.e., that they stay with the particular approach that seems to suit them.
2. Our use of personality drawn from traditional clinical usage contrasts with that of Allport (1937). Allport's concept of character is somewhat more inclusive than ours. He defined character as personality evaluated. He defined personality as "the dynamic organization within the individual of those psychophysical systems that determine his characteristic behavior and thought." Although we would include affective components, along with behavior and thought, as characteristically determined by character, we think of personality as distinctive, relatively abiding configurations separate from, although usually interrelated to, character.
3. We are using scheme and structure interchangeably.
4. It also ignores what seems apparent to us: that for any social animal it is not survival of the fittest that counts as much as survival of the group. It seems likely that those genes that support group or social functions are more powerful than those that support intellectual giftedness or strong forearms. It is likely that maturational factors are keyed to person objects. For example, affect may be tied to face configuration as suggested by Spitz (1965). Such a maturational

factor helps separate social from physical domains, although it is not necessary in order to construct these distinctions (Malerstein & Ahern, 1982). See Chapter 14 for a fuller discussion.

5. The intuitive phase and the symbolic phase make up the preoperational period. Phase is used by us in this book, in contrast to our earlier works, in order to be in keeping with Piaget's view that the symbolic and intuitive phases are not well-demarcated stages (Inhelder, personal communication).

6. Since it is more descriptive of a type of logic, we no longer exclude use of the term preconceptual as we did in our earlier work (Malerstein & Ahern, 1982).

7. We tend to use attribute, value, and quality interchangeably, because from a cognitive point of view all three words refer to properties of objects and events, although value generally has a greater social, hence affective, aspect. All three are essentially part objects.

8. We are assuming the child felt her mother to be competitive. It is equally possible in this instance for the child to feel that her mother wanted to be a part of her.

9. It should be noted that "I might be more persuasive if I understand his point of view" is a formal operational correction, a thinking about thinking (Malerstein & Ahern, 1982). Understanding his point of view serves intuitive goals (getting and having). We will address this later when we discuss treatment.

10. Obviously, being on his own is a matter of degree regardless of his interpretation, since no child may survive on his own.

11. When constraints are placed on the system by organic factors, or by repeated and repeatedly successful, patterned activity that works, i.e., schemes, then these constraints change the system. Better-working systems evolve. But this connecting of things, this assimilation, remains the natural tendency and may persist generally in certain individuals, even though under some circumstances a more differentiated system would work better.

12. Some adults take on as an identity the role of "treater." When psychotherapists do this they behave in all their social encounters as if they were doing psychotherapy. They

respond with empathy and acceptance to whatever another person says, regardless of the circumstances.

Another type of person may become the "treatment" or medicine for an emotionally ill caregiver. One child was adopted to help his mother recover from depression. The child's role was treatment. Later as part of the psychiatric profession, he molded himself to patients, becoming the treatment, often knowing how to respond, and not quite understanding how or what he knew.

13. As noted, if the overprotectiveness experienced is moderate, the child may become an operational with obsessive traits.

14. Negotiating with the physical world has an affective component, but once one learns not to bump into hard things or not to try to walk away with attractive things that are too heavy to lift, pain or frustration, i.e., affects, do not play substantial roles in these interactions.

15. Note how the quality of indecisiveness differed from that of the operational character in Chapter 5 who wanted to "toss his hat in the ring," who knew what he wanted, but was afraid.

16. This kind of erratic behavior is of course also consistent with an intuitive character's impulsivity.

17. The abstinent stance does not require the extremes practiced by many psychoanalysts in the 1950s when psychoanalysis-as-a-science was in full sway. Some psychoanalysts considered it a breach of technique to stand when the patient entered the consulting room, to say hello or goodbye, or to open the door for the patient, let alone to offer condolences for a death in the patient's family. All such activity on the part of the psychoanalyst was viewed as a violation of the pure laboratory setting in which transference phenomena could be analyzed. Many analysands could tolerate and even thrive on this stringent stance, which probably said as much about the psychoanalysts and their needs to be pure scientists as it did about the analysands.

18. See Malerstein and Ahern (1982) regarding the position that morality and convention are on the same continuum. See also the section on social-ego Chapter 4.

19. This type of learning is not in keeping with the psycho-

analytic conceptualization of insight, i.e., being affect-laden, including genetic roots and finally, core reorganization. Some psychoanalysts recommended insight as the treatment for persons whom they classified as having character disorders and whom we would classify as intuitives. These analysts proposed that internalization of aggressive impulses leads to depression and that when such internalized content is analyzed, the final result is superior to the pretreatment state. This point remains debatable although the rationale is understandable. Without doubt, these same analysts would not attempt this approach with those intuitive and symbolic characters who tend to show signs of acting out, severe depression, or psychosis following any undermining of defenses or development of an observing ego.

20. The counseling stance is characterized by a standing by or a ready-to-be-helpful quality, not a constant suggesting or teaching, but rather a tone that allows this experience to persist.

21. The Yochelson-Samenow (1976) approach to the criminal personality operates in the same medium, with the patient being guided or taught but with a condemnatory tone. The condemnatory side of the intuitive, which usually remains externally focused or projected, is partially introjected when this approach is successful. By our estimate, this approach works for 80% of the 10% of the criminal population who volunteer for treatment (not an insignificant accomplishment).

We think a similar approach works for certain intuitive symbolics, who then incorporate an identity as a bad person to solve their identity problem. This successful outcome appears to result from a transformation much like a religious conversion, as sometimes takes place in persons who embrace EST or Synanon.

22. The traits of the narcissistic personality correspond most closely to those of the intuitive character, whereas the traits of the borderline correspond to those of the symbolic character. However, most narcissistic personalities we find are intuitive symbolics. At the same time, the diagnosis of borderline personality is currently (DSM-III) made on the basis

of impulsive and narcissistic traits, excluding or neglecting those patients whom we would call operational symbolic. The original observations of Deutsch (1942), which predated the concept of borderline personality, would not have excluded operational symbolics.

23. See Note 1.

24. Masterson details his patient's themes and his own therapeutic interventions. Details are often lacking in other clinical literature. These details enable us to reinterpret Masterson's data.

25. We remind the reader that we formulated our concept of the symbolic character in part by extrapolating backward from our knowledge of the schizophreniform syndromes (Malerstein & Ahern, 1982). Hence in our analysis, although few symbolics are schizophrenic, all schizophrenics are symbolic.

26. Much shifting and struggle has taken place among psychoanalytic theoreticians regarding the theory of treatment. Friedman (1979) traced these changes beautifully. He concluded that the decision made at the 1961 Edinburgh Conference that insight through interpretation demarcated psychoanalysis and that cure through relationship was not psychoanalysis was too extreme. Friedman asserted that attachment (his term for therapeutic relationship) and integration, as well as insight, have always been a part of psychoanalytic treatment according to Freud. Friedman proposed that the introjection of the neutral object—the analyst—goes hand in hand with insight. Friedman used the Piagetian scheme to explain that the introjection of the neutral object, and insight or understanding are part of the same activity that allows construction of self and object as separate entities; this in turn leads to intrapsychic restructuring, an integration, Freud's third factor.

We think there is reason to define psychoanalysis as it was in Edinburgh. Not only is psychoanalysis thereby distinguished from other psychotherapeutic approaches but also there are some patients, operationals, who we think benefit most from insight, including insight into the transference, and are thus best treated by a neutral therapist.

27. In our previous work (Malerstein & Ahern, 1982) we dis-

cussed the struggle between the situationists and the individuists. For a time the situationists held the stronger position, contended that specifics of situations predicted
behavior, dismissing the 30% predictability of personality
traits. Individuists then fought back, asserting that a 30%
correlation of personality traits across situations merited respect. Most recently, statisticians working with complex
systems such as weather prediction, epidemiology, or even
the crumbling of a brick find standard statistical measures
unsatisfactory (Crutchfield, Farmer, Packard, & Shaw,
1986). The early errors that creep into a complex system
have such far-reaching impact that the most we can expect
as evidence for a causal relationship are occasional repeti-
tions of pattern. In effect, 30% predictability in complex systems appears to be reasonable proof that a causal connection
is obtained. Ninety percent predictability in such a system
perhaps should cause us to wonder if we are measuring
something peripheral to the system, instead of the system
itself. For example, in intelligence testing, for which there is
a high level of reliability, we may be measuring education or
acculturation rather than what we intuit as basic intelligence.

28. We do not distinguish the dynamic unconscious from the
preconscious. See Malerstein (1986).

29. Identification usually is thought of as unconscious, holistic
incorporation into the self-representation of qualities that
are part of an object-representation. For example, the patient starts to dress like and sound like his therapist. A
patient may consciously and deliberately imitate his therapist, but of course, a sharp line does not exist among classes
of activities based on consciousness, as there are many unconscious elements in any conscious imitation. Although
identification (imitation) may be classed as a defense mechanism, it is so powerful a device that it merits being singled
out.

30. It is unclear whether it is more useful to consider a defense
mechanism as a structure in itself or as merely a shift in the
relationship between structures, a nonaffective connec-
tivity. The fact that persons have preferred defenses based

on their character structure and personality suggests that such connectives are structures, and not just boundaries between two schemes.

31. See Malerstein (1986) for a discussion of neural patterns as schemes.

32. Obviously there are many substructures within the brain. Auditory, visual, touch, and motor areas are most obvious examples. These are demarcated physically from each other and provide certain boundaries to neural activity.

33. Spots or patches of light characterize the organization of incoming visual impulses to area 17, before the fibers to area 17 are fully myelinated.

34. Five or 6 months of experience occurs prior to the development of a line/edge-movement categorization of activity, allowing for assimilation of rich, undifferentiated cognitive–affective (social) schemes around ministrations and play. In lower animals, there is no such opportunity for interrelationships before the myelination to area 17 occurs (Malerstein, 1986).

35. If the formal operational reorganization seals the core, then our best opportunity for modifying the core is sometime in latency. It may be that to be truly effective, the focus in treatment of delinquents must be preadolescent, as in Project Re-ED (Hobbs, 1975), so that intervention may occur prior to whatever maturational factor ushers in a closing organization.

36. This is not in keeping with Stern's (1985) concept of Piaget's scheme as just an action scheme.

REFERENCES

Abraham, K. (1921). Contributions to the theory of the anal character. *Selected papers on psychoanalysis*. (D. Bryan & A. Strachey, Trans.). New York: Basic Books, 1960.

Ainsworth, M. D. S. (1982). Attachment: Retrospect and prospect. In C. M. Parkes & J. Stevenson-Hinde (Eds.), *The place of attachment in human behavior*. New York: Basic Books.

Alexander, F. (1948). *Fundamentals of psychoanalysis*. New York: Norton.

Allen, T. W., Walker, K., Symonds, L., & Marcell, M. (1977). Intrasensory and intersensory perception of temporal sequences during infancy. *Developmental Psychology, 13,* 225–229.

Allport, G. (1937). *Pattern and growth in personality*. New York: Holt, Rinehart & Winston.

Bahrick, L. E. (1988). Intermodal learning in infancy: Learning on the basis of two kinds of invariant relations in audible and visible events. *Child Development, 59,* 197–209.

Baker, H. S., & Baker, M. N. (1987). Heinz Kohut's self psychology: An overview. *The American Journal of Psychiatry, 144,* 1–9.

Bibring, E. (1953). The mechanisms of depression. In P. Greenacre (Ed.), *Affective Disorders*. New York: International Universities Press.

Bohart, A. C., & Henschel, D. M. (1984). Framework for a cognitive–developmental theory of psychopathology. In M. Paulsen & G. Lubin (Eds.), *Piagetian theory and its implications for mental health. Proceedings of Ninth through Twelfth Interdisciplinary Conference* (Vol II). Los Angeles: University of Southern California School of Education.

Bowlby, J. (1969). *Attachment and loss* (Vol. I). New York: Basic Books.

Bowlby, J. (1985). Developmental psychiatry comes of age. *American Journal of Psychiatry, 145:* 1–10.

Brenner, C. (1979). Working alliance, therapeutic alliance, and transference. *Journal of the American Psychoanalytic Association, 27* (Suppl.), 137–158.

Brown, T. A., & Weiss, L. (1982, January). *Some thoughts on Piaget's theory of affectivity*. Paper presented at the 12th Annual International Interdisciplinary Conference of Piagetian Theory and the Helping Professions, University of Southern California, Los Angeles, CA.

Case, R. (1980). *Vertical Decalage: A neo-Piagetian interpretation.* Paper presented at the tenth symposium of the Jean Piaget Society, Philadelphia, PA.

Crutchfield, J. P., Framer, J. D., Packard, N. H., & Shaw, R. S. (1986). Chaos. *Scientific American, 255,* 46–57.

Demany, L., McKenzie, B., & Vurpillot, E. (1977). Rhythm perception in early infancy. *Nature, 266,* 718–719.

Deutsch, H. (1942). Some forms of emotional disturbance and their relationship to schizophrenia. *Psychoanalytic Quarterly, 11,* 301–321.

Duckworth, E. (1983). Structures, continuity, and other people's minds. In K. Jervis (Ed.), *Reunion, reaffirmation and insurgence. Proceedings of the Miquon Conference on Progressive Education,* 48–60.

Eissler, K. (1953). The effect of the structure of the ego on psychoanalytic technique. *Journal of the American Psychoanalytic Association, 1,* 104–133.

Erikson, E. (1950). *Childhood and society.* New York: Norton.

Fantz, R. (1963). Pattern vision in newborn infants. *Science, 140,* 296–297.

Feffer, M. (1967). Symptom expression as a form of primitive decentering. *Psychological Review, 74,* 16–38.

Feffer, M. (1970). A developmental analysis of interpersonal behavior. *Psychological Review, 77,* 197–215.

Feffer, M. (1982). *The structure of Freudian thought: The problem of immutability and discontinuity in developmental theory.* New York: International Universities Press.

Field, T. M., Woodson, R., Greenberg, R., & Cohen, D. (1982). Discrimination and imitation of facial expressions by neonates. *Science, 218,* 179–181.

Fischer, K. W., & Pipp, S. L. (1983). Freudian thought in children and adults. *Contemporary Psychology, 28,* 280–282.

Freud, A. (1946). *The ego and the mechanisms of defense.* New York: International Universities Press.

Freud, S. (1943). *A general introduction to psychoanalysis.* Garden City, New York: Garden City Publishing.

Freud, S. (1959a). Recommendations for physicians on the psychoanalytic method. In *Sigmund Freud, collected papers, Vol. II* (J. Riviere, Trans.). New York: Basic Books.

Freud, S. (1959b). Further recommendations in the technique of psychoanalysis. In *Collected papers, Vol. II* (J. Riviere, Trans.). New York: Basic Books.

Freud, S. (1959c). Notes upon a case of obsessional neurosis. In *Collected papers, Vol. III* (A. Strachey & J. Strachey, Trans.). New York: Basic Books.

Freidman, L. Trends in the psychoanalytic theory of treatment. *Psychoanalytic Quarterly, 47,* 524–567.

Garrett, A. (1942). *Interviewing: Its principles and methods.* New York: Family Welfare Association of America.

Gill, M. (1954). Psychoanalysis and exploratory psychotherapy. *Journal of the American Psychoanalytic Association, 2,* 771–797.

Greenacre, P. (1954). The role of transference. *Journal of the American Psychoanalytic Association, 2,* 671–689.

Greenson, R. R. (1978). The working alliance and the transference neurosis. In

Explorations in psychoanalysis (119–224). New York: International Universities Press.

Greenwald, H. (1974). Treatment of the psychopath. In H. Greenwald, (Ed.) *Active psychotherapy* (pp. 363–377). New York: Jason Aronson.

Haith, M. M. (1980). *Rules that babies look by.* Hillsdale, NJ: Erlbaum.

Havens, L. (1986). *Making contact: Uses of language in psychotherapy.* Cambridge, MA: Harvard University Press.

Hill, L. B. (1955). *Psychotherapeutic interventions in schizophrenia.* Chicago: University of Chicago Press.

Hobbs, N. (1975). *The futures of children.* San Francisco, CA: Jossey Bass.

Hubel, D. H., & Weisel, T. N. (1979). Brain mechanism of vision. *Scientific American, 241,* 131–144.

Humphrey, K., Tees, R. C., & Werker, J. (1979). Auditory–visual integration of temporal relations in infants. *Canadian Journal of Psychology, 33,* 347–352.

Huszonek, J. J. (1987). Establishing therapeutic contact with schizophrenics: A supervisory approach. *American Journal of Psychotherapy, 41,* 185–193.

Inhelder, B., & Piaget, J. (1958). *The growth of logical thinking from childhood to adolescence.* (A. Parsons & S. Milgram, Trans.). New York: Basic Books.

Inhelder, B., & Piaget, J. (1969). *The early growth of logic in the child.* (E. Lunzer & D. Papert, Trans.). New York: Norton.

Inhelder, B., Sinclair, H., & Bovet, M. (1974). *Learning and the development of cognition.* Cambridge, MA: Harvard University Press.

Keller, E. F. (1978). Gender and science. *Psychoanalysis and contemporary thought, 1,* 409–433.

Kernberg, O. (1975). *Borderline conditions and pathological narcissism.* New York: Jason Aronson.

Kohlberg, L. A. (1963). The development of children's orientation toward a moral order: Sequence in development of moral thought. *Vita Humana, 6,* 11–33.

Kohut, H. (1977). *The restoration of the self.* New York: International Universities Press.

Langs, R., & Stone, L. (1980). *The therapeutic experience and its setting: A clinical dialogue.* New York: Jason Aronson.

Lecours, A. R. (1975). Myelogenetic correlates of the development of speech and language. In E. H. Lenneberg & E. Lenneberg (Eds.) *Foundations of language development: A multidisciplinary approach* (Vol. 1). New York: Academic.

Lippman, H. S. (1949). Difficulties encountered in psychiatric treatment of chronic juvenile delinquents. In K. R. Eissler (Ed.), *Searchlights on delinquency.* New York: International Universities Press.

MacFarlane, J. (1975). Olfaction in the development of social preferences in the human neonates. In M. Hofer (Ed.), *Parent–infant interaction.* Amsterdam: Elsevier.

Mahler, M. S. (in collaboration with M. Furer). (1968). *On human symbiosis and the vicissitudes of individuation. Infantile psychosis* (Vol. I). New York: International Universities Press.

Maier, H. W. (1965). *Three theories of child development.* New York: Harper and Row.

Main, M. (1987). *Cognitive aspects of attachment relationships.* Paper presented at

Seventeenth Annual Symposium of the Jean Piaget Society, Philadelphia, PA.

Malerstein, A. J. (1968). Depression as a pivotal affect. *American Journal of Psychotherapy, 22,* 202–217.

Malerstein, A. J. (1986). *The conscious mind.* New York: Human Sciences Press.

Malerstein, A. J., & Ahern, M. (1982). *A Piagetian model of character structure.* New York: Human Sciences Press.

Masterson, J. (1976). *Psychotherapy of the borderline adult: A developmental approach.* New York: Brunner/Mazel.

Masterson, J. (1985). *The real self: A developmental, self, and object relations approach.* New York: Brunner/Mazel.

Meltzoff, A. N., & Borton, W. (1979). Intermodal matching of human neonates. *Nature, 282,* 403–404.

Meltzoff, A. N., & Moore, M. K. (1977). Imitation of facial and manual gestures by human neonates. *Science,* October 8, 75–78.

Milgram, S. (1963). Behavioral study of obedience. *Journal of Abnormal and Social Psychology, 67,* 371–378.

Millar, S. (1968). *The psychology of play.* Baltimore, MD: Penguin Books.

Mounoud, P. (1977). *Sensori-motor development.* Paper presented at the Seventh Annual Symposium of Jean Piaget Society, Philadelphia: PA.

Murphy, P. (Ed.) (1985). *Recollections* (pp. 6–7). San Francisco, CA: *The Exploratorium.*

Piaget, J. (1937). Principle factors determining intellectual evolution from childhood to adult life. In *Factors determining human behavior* (Report of the Harvard Tercentary Conference of Arts and Sciences). Cambridge, MA: Harvard University Press.

Piaget, J. (1954). *The construction of reality in the child* (M. Cook, Trans.). New York: Basic Books.

Piaget, J. (1960). *The child's conception of physical causality* (M. Gabain, Trans). Patterson, NJ: Little Field, Adams.

Piaget, J. (1962). *Play, dreams, and imitation in childhood* (C. Gottegno & G. M. Hodgson, Trans.). New York: Norton.

Piaget, J. (1965a). *The moral judgment of the child* (M. Gabain, Trans.). New York: Free Press. (Originally published in 1932)

Piaget, J. (1965b). The child's conception of number. New York: Norton.

Piaget, J. (1971). *Structuralism* (C. Maschler, Ed. and Trans.). New York: Harper Torchbooks.

Piaget, J. (1973). *The child and reality: Problems of genetic psychology* (A. Rosin, Trans.). New York: Grossman.

Piaget, J. (1981a). *Intelligence and affectivity: Their relationship during child development* (T. A. Brown, & C. E. Kaegi, Eds. & Trans.). Palo Alto Annual Reviews Monographs.

Piaget, J. (1981b). Problems of equilibration. In J. M. Gallagher & D. K. Reid (Eds.), *The learning theory of Piaget and Inhelder* (E. Duckworth, Trans.). Monterey, CA: Brook/Cole.

Piaget, J., & Inhelder, B. (1969). *The psychology of the child* (H. Weaver, Trans.). New York: Basic Books.

Piattelli-Palmarini, M. (Ed.). (1980). *Language and learning: The debate between Jean Piaget and Noam Chomsky.* Cambridge, MA: Harvard University Press.

Pugh, G. E. (1977). *The biological origin of human values.* New York: Basic Books.

Russell, B. (1948). *Human knowledge.* New York: Simon and Schuster.

Sanford, N. (1948). *Psychology of motivation.* Course given at University of California, Berkeley.

Schachter, S., & Singer, J. E. (1971). Cognitive, social and physiological determinants of emotional state. *Psychoanalytical Review, 69,* 379–399.

Searles, H. F. (1965). Phases of patient–therapist interaction in the psychotherapy of chronic schizophrenia. In J. D. Sutherland (Ed.), *Collected papers on schizophrenia and related subjects.* New York: International University Press.

Shapiro, D. (1965). *Neurotic styles.* New York: Basic Books.

Siqueland, E. R., & DeLucia, C. A. (1969). Visual reinforcement of non-nutritive sucking in human infants. *Science, 165,* 1144–1146.

Spitz, R. (in collaboration with W. G. Cobliner). (1965). *The first year of life.* New York: International Universities Press.

Stern, D. N. (1985). *The interpersonal world of the infant.* New York: Basic Books.

Stone, M. *Transference and contact.* (1984). New York: Jason Aronson.

Volkan, V. D. (1976). *Primitive internalized object relations: A clinical study of schizophrenic, borderline, and narcissistic patients.* New York: International Universities Press.

Waldinger, R. J. (1987). Intensive psychodynamic therapy with borderline patients: An overview. *American Journal of Psychiatry, 144,* 267–274.

Weiss, J. (1967). The integration of defenses. *International Journal of Psychoanalysis, 48,* 520–524.

Wexler, B. E. (1986). A model of brain function, its implications for psychiatric research. *British Journal of Psychiatry, 148,* 351–362.

Windholz, E. (1957). Continuing Case Conference. San Francisco, CA: Langley Porter Institute.

Yochelson, S., & Samenow, S. E. (1976). *The criminal personality* (Vol. I). New York: Aronson.

Zetzel, E. R. (1971). A developmental approach to the borderline patient. *American Journal of Psychiatry, 127,* 867–871.

Zetzel, E. R. (1956). Current concepts of transference. *International Journal of Psychoanalysis, 37,* 369–378.

INDEX